D0041041

RETHINKING
THE
SALES
CYCLE

How Superior Sellers Embrace the
BUYING CYCLE
to Achieve a Sustainable and
Competitive Advantage

JOHN R. HOLLAND
TIM YOUNG

New York   Chicago   San Francisco   Lisbon
London   Madrid   Mexico City   Milan   New Delhi
San Juan   Seoul   Singapore   Sydney   Toronto

The *McGraw·Hill* Companies

1 2 3 4 5 6 7 8 9 0   DOC/DOC   0 1 0 9

ISBN: 978-0-07-163799-2
MHID: 0-07-163799-0

This publication is designed to provide accurate and authoritative information in regard to the subject matter covered. It is sold with the understanding that the publisher is not engaged in rendering legal, accounting, or other professional service. If legal advice or other expert assistance is required, the services of a competent professional person should be sought.

—From a declaration of principles jointly adopted by a committee of the American Bar Association and a committee of publishers.

FIgure 6-1 is from **The Social Technographics® of Business Buyers.** How Technology Buyers Engage with Social Media. February 20, 2009. This is the first document in the "B2B Social Media Strategy" series. By Laura Ramos, G. Oliver Young, with Peter Burris, Josh Bernoff, Bradford J. Holmes, Zachary Reiss-Davis. Reprinted with permission of Forrester Research, Inc.

McGraw-Hill books are available at special quantity discounts to use as premiums and sales promotions, or for use in corporate training programs. To contact a representative please visit the Contact Us pages at www.mhprofessional.com.

Library of Congress Cataloging-in-Publication Data

Holland, John R.
Rethinking the sales cycle : how superior sellers embrace the buying cycle to achieve a sustainable and competitive advantage / John Holland and Tim Young.

     p. cm.
  ISBN-13: 978-0-07-163799-2 (alk. paper)
  ISBN-10: 0-07-163799-0
  1. Selling. 2. Consumer behavior. 3. Sales management. I. Young, Tim. II. Title.
  HF5438.25.H639 2010
  658.85—dc22
                                   2009029686

To buyers everywhere who tolerate unrewarding buying experiences. Enlightened sales organizations will change their ways and align with how you want to buy. Selling is dead. Long live buying.

—John Holland

To my wife, Liz, the most beautiful person I've ever known and the source of all my happiness and inspiration.

To my mother, who always put me first.

—Tim Young

CONTENTS

FOREWORD, by Neil Rackham   VII

INTRODUCTION Why Read This Book?   XI

▰ PART 1   **The Power Has Moved to the Buyer**   1

CHAPTER 1   The Odd Couple   3

CHAPTER 2   Buyer's Revenge   27

▰ PART 2   **The Five Stages of the B2B Buying Cycle**   43

CHAPTER 3   Stage 1: Awareness and Urgency— Initiating the Buying Cycle   45

CHAPTER 4   Stage 2: Research   67

CHAPTER 5   Stage 3: Preferences   89

CHAPTER 6   Stage 4: Reassurance   105

CHAPTER 7   Stage 5: Risk—The Go/No-Go Buying Decision   123

■■ PART 3   **Fostering a Sales Culture That Facilitates Buying**   **139**

CHAPTER 8   How Traditional Selling Conflicts with the New Buying Process   **141**

CHAPTER 9   Getting Product Marketing Right   **155**

CHAPTER 10   Managing Sales to Facilitate the Buying Process   **177**

CHAPTER 11   MAGIC Moments: Creating a Great Customer Experience   **199**

CHAPTER 12   Using a Sales Process to Achieve a Sustainable Competitive Advantage   **215**

INDEX   **231**

Neil Rackham

It's exactly 20 years since I wrote *Major Account Sales Strategy*. The book opens with these words:

> *The measure of an effective selling strategy is how well it succeeds in influencing customer purchasing decisions. If we assess a strategy's success by its impact on customers, then it follows that the better we understand the customer decision process, the better our strategy will be. What counts is the customer.*

That was my book's unique contribution. It was the first time that anyone had done some reverse engineering of sales strategy by starting with how B2B customers want to buy. *Major Account Sales Strategy* took me 10 years of research, involved the observation and analysis of many thousands of customer interactions and, at one time, employed a team of 20 people working on the data collection and analysis. So, when I finally pulled this mountain of material together into a book, I hope you'll forgive me for thinking—20 years ago—that I was about to change the selling world. I honestly believed, in the way that naïve young revolutionaries so often do, that once people had read the book they would see the error of their ways and repent. I imagined that sales vice presidents all over the world would say, "Of course! We've been blind. Our so-called strategies have been based on how we want to sell, not on how our customers want to buy. Our whole approach must change."

It didn't happen quite like that. I can't deny that *Major Account Sales Strategy* was an influential work. However, I also can't deny that it has been disappointing to me that change has not come more quickly. In an average year I read a new sales book every week and I review several dozen manuscripts sent to me by hopeful authors wanting an endorsement. I am continually amazed at how many of these offerings make minimal mention of buyers or—worse—treat buyers as an inconvenience that complicates and slows the selling cycle. "Where's the customer?" I mutter under my breath. Most of these writers are a dismal advertisement for the selling profession. True that the old-style hard sell, where the customer is treated as either a fool or an enemy, has largely died a natural death. But in its place we have volumes of advice on more elaborate ways of "winning" at the buyer's expense. It would feel so good to bang some heads together and tell these writers a few simple truths. Customers are smart. They are more sophisticated than you are. They instantly see through any tricks, tactics, or techniques that have the faintest whiff of manipulation about them. You can probably tell that I feel passionately about this.

Which brings me to *Rethinking the Sales Cycle* by John Holland and Tim Young. When McGraw-Hill asked me to review their manuscript, I was cautious. It's true that Holland and Young have a good reputation and that I had heard clients speak well of them. But I've been caught that way before. I'll name no names, but many of the best-known sales gurus have written books that show a shameful disregard, or even contempt, for customers. So I began Chapter 1 of *Rethinking the Sales Cycle* with fairly modest expectations. To my delight, the book starts firmly on the customer's side of the table, showing how unhelpful stereotypes have contributed to unproductive selling behavior. The authors argue that in the past, sales cycles based on how the vendor wants to sell worked because vendors held more power than they do today. With the advent of the Internet and the information that it has put into the buyer's hands, this power has shifted. The reality today is that selling will fail if it is exploitive, manipulative, or based on how vendors want to sell. This means that most companies will have to rethink the steps of their sales process.

Holland and Young look in detail at the impact of the Internet. They provide a clear and lucid account of how the whole buying process has been transformed, and use examples to show convinc-

ingly why yesterday's selling models can't cope with today's empowered customers. In place of the old models, they propose new ones
based on how customers want to buy instead of on how companies
want to sell. This, you can readily imagine, is music to my ears.

Their buying cycle model starts with a three-stage buying model
that evolved out of selling behavior research that I conducted for Xerox
and IBM many years ago. Using this as a broad base for understanding how B2B customers buy, they go on to adapt it in the form of a
five-stage buying model. They explain each stage with plentiful examples. I have always found buying models to be the bedrock of any
sales strategy, so it's good to see how much thought has gone into
their five steps. Salespeople, in general, know too little about how customers buy, which makes this book especially welcome and overdue.

Did I mention that the book is unusual in another respect? It puts
forward a clear point of view on a sophisticated and complex topic.
That's not what makes it unusual. I know of many books that cover
complex topics of substance, like key account management or sales
compensation models. What's different about Holland and Young's
book is that it is delightfully well written. It's a sad truth that most
well-written sales books have nothing to say, while most sales books
of substance are boring beyond belief. It's refreshing to read one of
those rare books where the reader can enjoy both style and substance.

Finally, I like *Rethinking the Sales Cycle* for what I call "hidden
extras." Yes, it's a book about rethinking sales cycles based on how
customers want to buy—and a very good book at that. But it has those
extra pearls of wisdom that can turn a good book into a great book. It
has useful things to say about sales and marketing integration—a
really hot topic where most companies are struggling. There's a digres-
sion into Lovaglia's Law (go read about it) and on how the balance
between timing and urgency changes customer-decision criteria. They
have interesting insights into the flaws of product training, the misuse
of proposals, and the sins of product marketing. John Holland and
Tim Young have made a useful and readable contribution. I applaud
them for it.

WHY READ THIS BOOK?

Companies that are seeking competitive differentiators soon realize that product and price aren't sustainable for the long term. If you have a superior offering today, enjoy it while it lasts. A competitor's new announcement can turn things upside down virtually overnight. Once that happens, and it will, you will be in catch-up mode and will likely end up engaging in a lengthy game of tug-of-war during which your offering will alternate between being superior and being inferior. Even while it is superior, you won't win all the time. You can take comfort in knowing that you won't lose every deal when it is inferior.

As for cost or price, consider the advantages that Dell and WalMart reaped by leveraging supply chain technology before other competitors in their market segments did so. That advantage has now vaporized. Their stocks are no longer darlings of Wall Street because supply chain competency has become a prerequisite for retailers to be competitive. For business-to-business (B2B) sales organizations in particular, pricing advantages are difficult to sustain, as each opportunity brings its own set of special circumstances.

ATMs, outsourcing, offshore manufacturing, software as a service, and e-commerce are examples of approaches that provided competitive advantages to early adopters, but soon became standard for the mainstream market. Competitive advantages are fleeting, unless you have something that is truly unique and inimitable. Since few vendors enjoy that position, how can you create a sustainable competitive advantage?

One approach is to become a moving target by developing a great offering and using it as a platform for developing your next great offering, leaving unaware, ill-equipped, or less visionary competitors constantly in catch-up mode. Apple has mastered this approach with its redesigned and innovative computers, iPods, and now iPhones. Again, few companies seem to be successful in executing such a strategy. How can companies with more ordinary offerings develop a sustainable competitive advantage that makes customers not only want to buy from them, but enjoy the process at the same time?

Sales Process as a Competitive Advantage

Many "buying experiences" ultimately are unpleasant for buyers. You need to look no further than buying a car or purchasing insurance for examples. But what if a company had a way to create superior buying experiences that made customers want to buy from it? Now that would be a sustainable differentiator! But can this be done?

For an example of how to create these memorable buying experiences, consider Disney. Disney is, of course, not the cheapest form of family entertainment. Parents dig deep for the experience, and the experience they receive is memorable and favorable, as Disney has long been committed to an ongoing training culture that allows its representatives to create "magic moments" for its customers. Perhaps this explains why Disney is perennially one of the most admired companies in America. For decades, Disney has consistently delivered superior customer experiences.

Now compare this to how your customers perceive you, or how they perceive your competitors. For that matter, think of your own buying experiences and which, if any, stand out as being superior. *Facilitating great buying experiences for your customers may be the most sustainable, defensible competitive advantage that you can hope for.* It will be difficult for your competitors to imitate, while creating tremendous brand value for you. It can make your marketing easier, create lasting relationships with customers, and make your company a very desirable place to work. It starts and ends with the customer, and if you can create a process, a culture, and a system for consistently facilitating great buying experiences, you will be unbeatable.

This book aims to show you how to achieve this lofty goal.

Understanding How People Buy

When people are making buying decisions, basic human emotions rule the day. Despite this reality, traditional sales training and approaches, whether internally developed or provided by outside vendors, have in the past and continue today to cast a blind eye to how people buy. Research has shown that buyers exhibit predictable behavior when ordering from a menu, buying a house, or purchasing enterprise software.

How many times have you seen buyers

- Make an impulse purchase, and later try to defend or justify it with logic?

- Offer a valid objection, only to have a salesperson attempt to trivialize it?

- Dwell on the negative aspects of what they consider to be their best alternative just before making a buying decision?

- Offer an objection that a seller cannot and, more important, should not try to address?

- Learn the price of an item and allow a salesperson to continue selling, despite having already decided that it was too expensive and the sale was not going to happen?

- Decide not to buy because a seller attempted to close too soon or too aggressively?

- Express reservations about making a purchase, only to be reassured and closed multiple times?

- Feel that a salesperson was attempting to control or dominate them during a sales call?

The manner in which sellers read and react to these situations goes a long way toward shaping the buying experience.

Superior sellers align with human buying behavior during sales cycles, but they do it intuitively rather than deliberately. For that reason, it is a skill that cannot readily be transferred. Salespeople and their organizations constantly look ahead at opportunities in their pipelines as they face unrelenting quota pressure. By failing to analyze past buyer behavior in successes and failures, opportunities to understand and improve are lost.

This book has been written to be agnostic concerning any particular sales methodology until late in the book. Regardless of your prior sales experience or training, it will provide a better understanding of the mindset, emotions, and behaviors of buyers as they progress through five stages of a buying cycle. (Throughout the book, the term *sales cycle* has been replaced with *buying cycle*. Making that simple change shifts the focus to buyers rather than the traditional view of closing deals.)

As you read, we encourage you to map your selling activities, whether they are self-taught or based upon a sales methodology, to the way human beings buy. Also consider past buying or selling situations that you've experienced to validate the buying behaviors described in the book. You will gain insight into

- How buyers' priorities changes as they go through buying cycles

- The five stages of a buying cycle

- The power that customers have, via word of mouth, to build or kill your business

- A way to redefine selling to improve alignment with buyers

- How and when buying cycles begin

- Why some buying cycles end unsuccessfully

- The different implications that buyer objections have depending upon when in the buying cycle they are raised

- How to take a committee through a buying cycle to maximize the chance of consensus at the end

- How to interpret buying behavior at different stages

- Assessing your competitive position at different stages based upon buyer behavior

- How to merge your selling process with a buyer's buying process

Buyer Behavior Is Predictable

Unfortunately, for most organizations, so is selling behavior, and it often conflicts with the way buyers want to be treated. This gives you a golden opportunity. Understanding and reacting in a way that aligns with buyers can be a sustainable differentiator for you or your organization.

John Holland and Tim Young

PART 1

The Power Has Moved to the Buyer

THE ODD COUPLE

A buyer and a seller make for a really odd couple. When you think about it, buyers and sellers should be highly compatible. After all, their relationship *should* exist solely because each party can help the other to get something it wants. A buyer may want something tangible—a new phone system, perhaps. A seller of phone systems wants the buyer to have the phone system, because the act of satisfying that need consummates a sale. Ah, and, conveniently enough, it is through this transaction that the seller earns her pay-check in the form of a commission. It's also through this transaction that the seller's company realizes revenue, which leads to increased earnings and, if well managed, increased shareholder value in the form of rising stock prices. And all of that can reflect positively on the seller, who may earn herself a trip to President's Club or some other incentive program that her company has in place for top performers.

But something is wrong in the relationship between buyers and sellers, and has been for a long time. While both parties appear to have a common agenda, they are inherently focused on different outcomes, and each is suspicious of the other's agenda. Buyers want to achieve goals, solve problems, and satisfy needs. Most sellers want (or are perceived by buyers to want) to sell something. Anything. Generally, they want to deliver the best combination of high price and quick sale so that they can move on to . . . the next sale. And they have an entire company behind them encouraging (pressuring?) them to do so for all the financial reasons mentioned earlier.

Why the disconnection between the two? The answer in this case is simple. Stereotypical sellers are perceived as putting the sales first and the buyer's needs second. Repairing the relationship, of course, will prove to be more difficult and will take a lot of work. And this is not one of those relationships where both parties share equal blame. In this relationship, the seller is largely at fault and, as a result, must shoulder the responsibility for treating buyers in a more honorable way. Actually, we'll go further than that and suggest that sellers' organizations should accept responsibility for having fostered cultures focused on "driving sales" rather than on ensuring "great customer experiences." After all, there are no incentive trips (to our knowledge) for salespeople who ensure great customer experiences.

In the buy/sell transaction, only one party's compensation is tied to the transaction, and that's the seller's. And this is at the heart of the disconnection in the relationship. The seller has to make the sale, or she doesn't eat.

Abraham Maslow, in his 1943 paper "A Theory of Human Motivation," described five levels of human needs (see Figure 1.1). The theory is that humans must satisfy each level of needs before they can progress to the next level. Naturally, the most fundamental level relates to surviving. Can I breathe? Do I have food and water? Where can I find shelter?

Source: Abraham Maslow, *Motivation and Personality*, 2nd ed. (New York: Harper & Row, 1970).

SELF-
ACTUALIZATION
Pursue Inner Talent
Creativity Fulfillment

SELF-ESTEEM
Achivement Mastery
Recognition Respect

BELONGING – LOVE
Friends Family Spouse Love

SAFETY
Security Stability Freedom from Fear

PHYSIOLOGICAL
Food Water Shelter Warmth

Figure 1-1 *Abraham Maslow's Hierarchy of Needs*

In our modern business world, we meet many of our physiological needs by earning a paycheck. For better or worse, gone are the days when we lived off the land, built our own homes, grew our own food, sewed our own clothes, and generally provided for ourselves. Today, our paychecks allow us to pay rent or a mortgage (shelter), buy groceries (food), and pay the heating bill (warmth). This allows us to meet most of our physiological needs, so naturally we turn our attention to the next level, safety. Again, in our modern world, this is less about physical protection than it was a hundred years ago and more about protection of the things we have that allow us to meet our physiological needs—the house we rent, the ability to buy food, the clothes we wear, and so on. And what's the one thing we must have in order to protect all of those things? Job security and a paycheck. If you're a seller, you get that only if you are successful in *making sales*, and that's not at all likely to change. Nor do we propose that it should. What we will propose in this book is a way to achieve an increased awareness of the needs, wants, and roles of each party and a set of behavioral changes, both individually and organizationally, that will result in not only increased sales, but, much more importantly, more positive customer experiences. And that's the foundation of a healthy and mutually rewarding relationship.

The Buyer's View of the Seller

Buyers' relationships with salespeople run the gamut. A small percentage of sellers display extraordinary sincerity and competence. Buyers value their opinions and view them as respected advisors. In these situations, the buyer's experience is outstanding, largely because the buyer feels that buying rather than selling is the focus. Unfortunately, the majority of relationships are more stereotypical, with buyers feeling that sellers are trying to push offerings onto them. They view salespeople as following the old adage of "when all you have is a hammer, everything looks like a nail." Buyers have to deal with sellers who conduct themselves in this manner.

You can get a sense for a typical buyer-seller relationship by considering that many terms used by sales organizations are also used during military engagements: win, lose, campaign, beachhead, and so on. Sun Tzu's *The Art of War* is required reading for some sales organizations and is referenced to devise selling strategies. Trite phrases are passed along in sales meetings that show blatant disrespect for buyers. The implication is that not only can buyers be manipulated, but they *should* be manipulated! Some typical phrases:

"Selling begins when the buyer says no."

"Buyer objections are selling opportunities."

"Winners never quit and quitters never win."

"Don't confuse the sell with the install."

"Selling is learning the ABC's: Always Be Closing."

These attitudes and approaches contribute to the fact that for the last several decades, the buyer-seller relationship has been at best strained, and at worst broken. Contrary to common belief, salespeople are not entirely responsible. It may be in retaliation for having been "wronged" in the past, but there are occasions when buyers manipulate salespeople. One example is inviting sellers to bid on RFPs that they have virtually no chance of winning, yet that they will have to invest a lot of their time and their companies' resources to respond to. The sole purpose of soliciting these bids is for buyers to gain negotiating leverage with the vendor that wired and will almost certainly be awarded the RFP. When asked, buyers tell other salespeople: "This RFP is wide open. Whoever has the best offering will win. If you can get your foot in the door, there are many upcoming requirements. We've heard good things about your company and look forward to seeing your bid." Buyers suffer no pangs of regret when they lie to salespeople. Turnabout is fair play.

Through the years, buyers of business-to-business (B2B) offerings and services have controlled the beginning and end of sales cycles. Buyers decide whether or not they are willing to meet with or take a phone call from a salesperson. When issuing an RFP, the vendors that can bid are by invitation only. Buyers also control the purse strings by deciding whether to buy and then selecting which vendor at the end of the buying cycle.

Perhaps because they resent this control, sellers display some of their most aggressive and obnoxious behavior in these two parts of the buying cycle. They are persistent in trying to gain access despite obstacles (gatekeepers, unreturned voice mails, and so on). To buyers, these efforts may appear more along the lines of stalking than of prospecting. Sellers also have a reputation for saying whatever is necessary to get prospects to part with their money at the end of the sales cycle by utilizing high-pressure closing techniques.

The Quest for Control

Despite these conflicting agendas, there is one area where buyers and sellers can agree. When asked to define selling, even though the parties are on opposite sides of the desk, they use the same words and phrases. Their descriptions include elements of conflict or confrontation:

- Convincing

- Persuading

- Handling/overcoming objections

- Manipulating

- Haggling

We're not sure how this definition came to be, but unless one or both sides modify their views and behavior, buyer-seller relationships aren't going to change anytime soon.

Later in this book, we'll offer an alternative definition of selling that can be a first step in reducing buyer-seller tension, but for now we hope you agree that the lines are clearly drawn. Buyers view selling as something that is done to them rather than for or with them. The predictable result is that buyers don't like to be sold and prefer to avoid talking to new salespeople. Until recently, however, when considering complex offerings, buyers had no choice but to engage with salespeople.

The reason for this is that prior to the Internet, B2B selling organizations exerted control over information. If buyers wanted to learn about the latest offerings and industry trends, they had to schedule sales calls. If several buyers within an organization were interested, a presentation could be arranged so that the group could learn about what offerings were available in the marketplace. Salespeople took these invitations for granted, but they gave the seller a significant advantage. They allowed salespeople to be involved during the very early stages of the sales cycle. Buyers were blank canvases, and therefore salespeople had significant influence in determining or shaping their requirements. Competent sellers were able to do this with a bias toward their offerings to make things difficult for any competitors that might be brought in later.

Whether you are grading salespeople, carpenters, lawyers, or consultants, a general rule applies: about 10 percent are exceptional, 80 percent fall within a vast middle range, and 10 percent either are or border on being incompetent. Why is there such a pervasive negative stereotype of salespeople? It probably stems from prior negative experiences during business-to-consumer (B2C) interactions before people rose to positions in companies and got involved in B2B buying decisions.

Think for a moment and recall some of your most unpleasant interactions with salespeople. Some are so bad that people who otherwise wanted to buy couldn't do so because the seller was so pushy or obnoxious. That is how strongly a seller can affect a buyer. Out of ten sellers you deal with, if nine are okay or better, human nature is such that you remember the worst one. This is the major reason that the pervasive negative stereotype of salespeople exists.

We wanted to provide a few representative examples of regrettable buying experiences.

Buying a First New Car

A year after starting his first real job, Sam decided that it was time to get rid of his old car and realized that, for the first time, he could afford a new car. He visited a dealership to choose the model, determine the options on the car that would fit his needs and budget, and place an order. The car he was replacing had over 140,000 miles on the odometer, and the salesperson suggested that he sell it privately because it would be difficult to give much of a trade-in allowance for it. That prompted Sam to ask when the new car would come in, and the seller indicated that it would be delivered in six weeks. Sam asked a second time, telling the salesperson that he was not in a rush and would be willing to wait longer if necessary. The seller gave him his word that it would take six weeks.

A month later, Sam called to explain that he was going to begin the grim task of placing an ad to try to sell his old car and wanted to verify the delivery date. The response was that in two weeks or less, he'd be driving the shiny new car. After meeting numerous sketchy people and suffering through a few harrowing test drives, he found someone who was anxious to buy the car, agreed on a price, and placed a deposit. He waited a full week past when Sam had told him he could have the car, but finally he couldn't wait any longer. Sam apologized profusely and refunded his deposit.

The new car arrived ten weeks after the delivery date that had been confirmed three different times. When he was told that the car was in, Sam explained that in light of all the trouble he had gone through, the salesperson would have to take his old car for something approaching what he had it sold for, only to have the sale fall through. The seller mumbled that the dealership would step up and do the right thing, so Sam test-drove the car and was delighted with it.

At this point, the salesperson told him that there had been a price increase and that the dealership couldn't honor the original purchase price because it would lose money. Sam quickly recognized a transparent attempt to manufacture a trade-in allowance on the old car and was infuriated. He told the salesperson to do something with the new car that was physically impossible and stormed out of the showroom.

Within a day, Sam found a used car that was a much more attractive option and bought it. The salesperson from the dealership called the next day to try to smooth things over. He was willing to honor the original price and give a trade-in allowance. Once again Sam reiterated his advice about what to do with the car.

Buying any car, especially your first new car, should be a joyful occasion, but a pushy, obnoxious, or deceitful salesperson often finds a way to rain on a buyer's parade.

Buying a Big-Screen TV

To better understand a buyer's view of selling, imagine visiting a retail store to buy a new television when you have limited knowledge about what's available. A clerk approaches and asks: "May I help you?" Despite the buyer's desperate need for assistance, the most common answer is: "No. I'm just looking." Why do buyers respond this way? They distrust salespeople who haven't demonstrated that they are different from the negative stereotype. They don't want their decision to be influenced by sellers who may not have their best interests at heart. By the way, this may be a completely false concern in that many sellers are making an earnest effort to help you determine what you need. Having said that, everyone who has been burned before carries that experience into each encounter with a new salesperson.

After a frustrating 15 minutes of wandering through the store looking at TVs, you leave, feeling more confused than enlightened. (How big? LCD? Plasma? Projection? How do I decide which one?) When you return home, a neighbor hears about your experience and gives you a copy of the latest *Consumer Reports* with evaluations and recommendations of new televisions. You read the entire article and determine that a 46-inch, LCD, 1080p, JVC television is the best option available for what you want to spend. You are comfortable with your decision because you believe that *Consumer Reports* is a competent, unbiased source that has no financial interest in or potential gain from whatever decision you make.

Armed with this knowledge, you revisit the same store and are approached by another clerk, who asks: "May I help you?" This time, you respond: "Yes. I want to buy a 46-inch, LCD, 1080p, JVC television." Why is your response different from that on your initial visit? You know what you want, and you will not have to be subjected to a salesperson's efforts to influence your requirements. With this knowledge, you view the seller's role as that of a buying facilitator—someone who is going to help you buy what you have already determined is best for your needs. Potential buyer-seller tension is minimized unless the seller tries to talk you out of the decision you've made. Having said that, despite the seller's touting the great reliability of the TV you choose, be prepared for the attempted upsell of an extended warranty.

Human Buying Behavior

Just as they have for air, water, food, and shelter, humans have an innate desire for control. When they are buying, people are in control. They set a budget, decide what their needs are, and take action to satisfy them. Buying feels good! Being sold means that a salesperson with a financial incentive is attempting to convince, persuade, or influence your decision. Buyers who have been taken advantage of, manipulated, and pressured in the past don't want to allow the seller to be in control.

We would like to share some insights into human buying behavior with you. In 1979, Mike Bosworth, a cofounder of CustomerCentric Selling and author of the 1994 book *Solution Selling: Creating Buyers in Difficult Selling Markets*, was working for Xerox Computer Services (XCS). As a small division of Xerox ($120 million in sales, 100 new business reps, 20 managers), XCS wanted to implement a sales methodology and hired Neil Rackham as a consultant to support those efforts. Rackham was an experimental psychologist who had been working with companies such as Xerox and IBM to develop new sales models based on research that measured differences in behavior between high-performing and average-performing salespeople.

At Xerox, Rackham and his team had observed over 1,500 sales calls to identify seller behaviors that resulted in positive reactions from buyers. During this research they developed models of what made individual sales calls successful. Xerox had been using these models to train their divisions that sold copiers, fax machines, training services, and word processors.

Ultimately, XCS struggled to implement the new process. The reason? XCS was selling a disruptive technology—hosted first-generation material requirements planning (MRP) systems. Most buyers in the manufacturing market had no clue about the breakthrough capabilities that XCS was offering. The XCS sale was considerably more complex than the average copier sale.

Over dinner, Neil and Mike discussed these difficulties. Neil shared what he had learned from his research into long-cycle sales at Xerox and other corporations. He shared with Mike the four factors that he had found to be important to buyers during buying cycles. He had discovered that as buyers went through the three phases of a buying cycle that he defined, the importance of those factors varied. These three phases are shown in Figure 1-2, which we'd like to describe in detail for you. Incidentally, at the time of this conversation, neither Rackham nor Bosworth was well known in the selling world. Mike Bosworth went on to develop Solution Selling, incorporating this chart into his work, while Neil Rackham was to become widely known for his books, including *SPIN Selling* and *Major Account Sales Strategy*, both published by McGraw-Hill.

These shifting buyer concerns, which we refer to as "buying curves," show the change in buyers' focus as they navigate through buying cycles. These buying curves can be confusing, even overwhelming, when you first look at them. Let us first explain the mechanics and structure and then, using a typical B2C buying experience, explore the nuances.

How Buyers Buy

When we analyzed the original research, we determined that buyers typically go through three distinct phases as they move through their buying cycle.

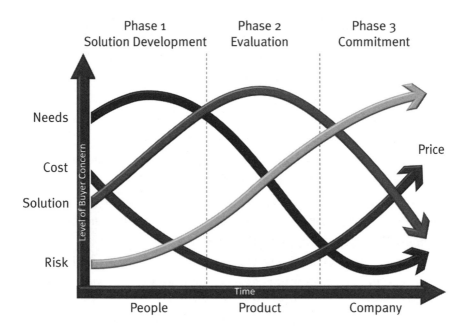

Figure 1-2 *Shifting Buyer Concerns*

Phase 1 of the buying cycle is the need development or solution development phase. This phase commences when the buyer recognizes that he has a goal, problem, or need that he feels should be addressed. In fact, as we'll discuss later in the book, buyers typically exist at one of three levels of need at any given point in time: latent need, active need, or vision. Phase 1 of the buying cycle starts when the buyer makes the transition from a latent need (i.e., something that he did not previously realize that he should be focusing on) to an active need. Phase 1 concludes when the buyer has a clear vision of the capabilities that he thinks he needs in order to achieve his goal, solve his problem, or satisfy his need.

Phase 2 of the buying cycle is the evaluation or proof phase. During Phase 2, the buyer seeks to validate his vision and determine if there is a vendor that can, in fact, meet his requirements (or if it's something that he can do on his own).

Phase 3 of the buying cycle is the commitment phase. Once a buyer (or buying committee) has successfully navigated the first two phases (i.e., he has established an active need to be addressed and validated that an offering can meet his requirements), he begins evaluating whether or not, given all of his other priorities, this is in fact something that he should decide to purchase.

In addition to the three distinct phases that focus on the timing aspect of a buying decision (the x axis), there are four key areas of concern that the buyer also takes into account: needs, cost/price, solution, and risk (the y axis). The research has shown us that as buyers navigate buying cycles, these four areas take on varying degrees of significance in their minds.

Let's explore each of these areas of concern using the following B2C buying example that one of our colleagues experienced.

And Baby Makes Three

In October 1993, after two years of marriage, Frank's wife informed him that there would be an additional member joining their family in nine months. At the time, they lived in a lovely lakefront condo with a boat dock only 20 feet from the back door. Boating in the summer, ice skating in the winter, and sunset cruises up the lake to a great little restaurant in other months kept their leisure life active and exciting. But there was a problem . . . two, actually. First of all, they had only two bedrooms, one of which was Frank's home office. More important, his wife became convinced that their little bundle of joy would one day wander out the back door and fall in the lake. Time to sell the lake house.

Phase 1: Need for New Accommodations

This was Frank's Phase 1. He suddenly found himself in need of new accommodations, and he had quickly gone from a latent need (no kids) to an active need (get ready). So, being the conscientious buyers they were, Frank and his wife sat down to define their requirements. They began the process by asking each other questions, such as

- How many bedrooms will we need?

- How much land would we ideally like?

- What about the school system? Is that a factor?

- Do we need a fenced yard?

- What about a pool?

- Do we need room for a home office?

- Do we want to be closer to or further away from our families?

- What can we afford?

- What price do we need to get for the condo?

The questions continued over the course of several discussions until they had what they thought was their "ideal" list of requirements. They had navigated Phase 1 by focusing on their needs and defining those requirements (the first buyer curve). Cost was a concern, but not as great a one as their needs. In fact, as they brainstormed their ideal home, their sensitivity to cost became less and less of an issue (the second buyer curve). It was still just talk at this point, so the "solution" (i.e., the actual house) was still just a dream, not a physical address (the third buyer curve). Accordingly at this phase, risk was low. They were just beginning to shop.

Phase 2: Open House Hell

Once they had agreed on their vision, it was time for them to determine if that vision could, in fact, be fulfilled. They entered into Phase 2.

Their concern with the refinement of their requirements (the first buyer curve) began to lose its focus as they made the transition into trying to determine if there was, in fact, a house that would meet their needs (buyer curve three). As they spent weekends being led around to various prospective properties, their focus on cost (the second buyer curve) diminished as well. With each new and better offering they saw (the solution curve), their concern with the escalating numbers somehow took a backseat to fulfilling that vision.

As the reality of potentially making the major life change of buying a new house became more real, however, their sense of risk began to inch up. Should they really be having a baby and moving at the same time? Once they found a house that met all of their requirements, their proof was provided, and risk really started to escalate (notice the correlation between the peak of the solution curve and the increase in the escalation of the risk curve in the middle of Phase 2). Once they had found their dream home, reality began to set in. They might actually have to buy something!

They began asking themselves some preliminary risk questions, such as

• What if their offer wasn't accepted?

• What if it was?

• What if they couldn't get financing?

• Did they have any leverage if they had to negotiate?

How did they answer these questions? By having a Plan B and a Plan C. Specifically, by having a backup house or two in the queue in case something went wrong with their purchase of the one they really wanted. They created their "short list." There was a clear House A— the one that met most of their requirements. However, they had also found a couple of others, House B and House C, that they'd be able to live with in case their first choice fell through. When it came time to request a home inspection, however, the only house they were willing to invest that much time and money in was House A.

Phase 3: Decision Time

It was getting late in the process. The home inspection was done. House A was only about 10 percent more than their budget—not great, but manageable. It was time to make a decision. What were they thinking about at that point?

- Do we really *need* to do this now?

- Frank had just started his own business and didn't know if he was going to make it or go back into the corporate world. Is now the right time?

- The housing market looks like it's getting a little soft. Should we wait to see if we could get a better price?

Late in the buying process, risk (the fourth buyer curve) and price (the third buyer curve) were tantamount. In fact, these factors were so pronounced that they overshadowed both their needs (the first buyer curve) and the house they were seriously considering (the second buyer curve).

Ultimately, after several sleepless nights and more than one argument, their needs won out, but only after their risk was mitigated by a minor price concession on the part of the seller that involved including the washer/dryer and refrigerator as part of the deal.

This typical example of a major personal buying experience may help you to understand and validate the buying curves as they relate to a real estate transaction. The research indicated that people go through this process in making nearly all buying decisions: houses, cars, new computers, and even ordering from a menu. How often is your next to last hurdle before ordering the filet mignon "risk" (cholesterol), and if you pass that hurdle, the last one is the "price" ($34.00)? We'd now like to relate the buying curves to buying behavior during a B2B enterprise sale.

During Phase 1 of the buying curves, a buyer's needs are of paramount importance. They rank high to start with, and their importance increases through the middle of Phase 1. The advantage of initiating buying cycles is that the first vendor (Column A) has the best opportunity to influence the buyer's requirements. Competent sellers highlight their strengths and the potential weaknesses of vendors that may later be invited to compete. Note that the importance of cost lessens as the buyer's needs are developed. If the buyer starts to see potential value as the seller diagnoses her current situation, concerns about cost lessen.

This supports the psychology behind a major sales blunder. Salespeople are told (if not shown how) not to lead with product. Early in Phase 1, if the seller mentions the product, it is very likely that the buyer's next question will be, "How much does it cost?" The seller then faces some unattractive choices:

1. Try to deflect the conversation elsewhere, but run the risk of appearing slick.

2. Give a low number so as not to scare the buyer off.

3. Give a best-guess estimate.

4. Explain that it is early in the process, and it is necessary to better understand the buyer's requirements. If the buyer persists, give a range or a "not to exceed" figure that will probably be higher than the final quote.

The problem is that since the seller has not established value, almost any figure is going to seem high to the buyer. The longer a seller can defer pricing and establish value, the less price-sensitive the buyer will be, as shown in the cost curve in Phase 1. In a B2B sale, Phase 1 ends when a buyer knows her requirements and has a good idea of the estimated cost of the offering.

If a seller is the first vendor to talk with a buyer who has not been looking, the ideal outcome is that the requirements list becomes a mirror image of Column A's offering. As you can see in Figure 1-3, this means that sellers that are brought in later are going to be in reactive or defensive mode because the buyer is already in Phase 2. Column A will win the vast majority of these opportunities.

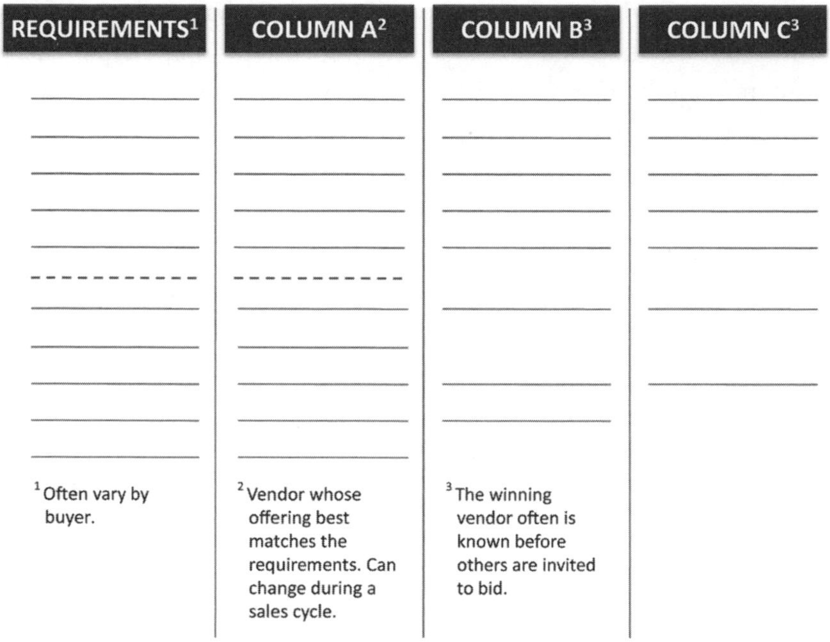

REQUIREMENTS[1]	COLUMN A[2]	COLUMN B[3]	COLUMN C[3]

[1] Often vary by buyer.

[2] Vendor whose offering best matches the requirements. Can change during a sales cycle.

[3] The winning vendor often is known before others are invited to bid.

Figure 1-3 *Vendor Evaluation*

During Phase 2, the most important issue is the solution, or match to the requirements. This is a time when proof (demonstrations, reference visits, white papers, and so on) becomes important because buyers want to verify that what the seller has articulated is achievable. Things that buyers see in offerings can alter what they feel is needed and change the requirements list during Phase 2. This is also a time when buyers will start to look at some competitive alternatives. The seller whose offering best matches the buyer's requirements is what we refer to as Column A. Risk starts to increase as a buyer evaluates alternatives; cost is not an issue provided there is potential value and other vendors are in the ballpark.

When Column A initiates an opportunity, many buyers get most of the way through Phase 2 before other vendors are invited to compete. Often Columns B, C, and so on, are not given adequate time to fully understand the buyer's requirements and make a detailed rec-ommendation. The primary reason they are invited to bid is to allow buyers to gain leverage that they can use to ensure that Column A provides an acceptable price.

Phase 2 ends when buyers (or buying committees) choose what they feel is the best alternative. If you're fortunate enough to be their choice (Column A), you may encounter a buyer whose behavior changes dramatically. A buyer may raise risk items (analogous to the house inspection) and go negative on the vendor he feels is the best alternative. Risk is seen only by Column A and is a good sign, as it indicates that the buyer is seriously considering buying your offering.

Sellers often misinterpret this change in behavior and panic. They see a person who has been very positive suddenly start challenging what they are proposing. Sellers may assume that these sudden con-cerns are an indication that another vendor has gained favor. This can cause the seller to try to address risk objections that it can't actually address (concerns about the economy, whether this is the right time, and so on). That can reduce the seller's credibility and actually heighten risk. The absolute worst thing a seller can do is to start dis-counting. At this stage, the buyer isn't concerned about cost; he's known that for some time. Rather, he is concerned about whether he will achieve what he wants to achieve with the offering.

Discounting actually validates a buyer's objections risk and is analogous to throwing gasoline on a smoldering fire. It can be viewed as agreeing with the concerns about risk and trying to mitigate them with discounting. The buyer is actually looking for empathy and reas-surance, if possible. If buyers show concern about risk, it will be seen only by Column A (the only vendor they are about to buy from), and at that point misbehaving can cause a seller to lose a sale that was hers to win.

A strange thing happens if the buyer successfully overcomes risk concerns and becomes ready to buy. At this point, the person you saw who was confused and undecided about pulling the trigger has a sud-den personality change. Once the buyer is past risk, price now becomes the issue, and he will beat the seller like a rented mule to get the best possible deal. Cost is what a buyer is willing to pay. Price is trying to ensure that he is getting the best deal.

As shown in the chart, during Phase 1, people (sales and support staff) are the most important influencers. During Phase 2, the offering is the star of the show, as the buyer has to verify in some fashion that the commitments made can be delivered. In Phase 3, the company becomes important. The majority of buyers are more comfortable doing business with vendors that have a strong track record and balance sheet. Smaller vendors or start-ups need a significant price/performance advantage when competing with perceived industry leaders, especially for conservative mainstream market buyers.

By understanding this behavior, sellers can better align with buyers. Let's see how this can put an objection into clearer perspective. First, try to determine where the buyer is in the buying phases. An objection means different things depending upon where the buyer is:

- A Phase 1 objection means that the buyer is trying to determine whether a feature is needed and should be one of the requirements.

- A Phase 2 objection means that the buyer is wondering if that feature will work in her environment.

- In Phase 3, an objection can be used as a negotiating ploy. The buyer could highlight a competitor's feature to indicate an area where your offering is not as strong.

Please note that the figure showing the buyer's requirements is oversimplified in that it may not represent a committee's view. It is likely that different committee members may have different Column A's for different reasons. The best strategy is to own the requirements list for the higher levels in the committee.

Committee sales (those with more than one person involved) are also challenging. If you have a three-person committee of equals with one buyer wondering what the firm needs (Phase 1), another wondering which vendor is the best choice (Phase 2), and the third concerned about what can go wrong if we go with Column A (Phase 3), that opportunity may not be closable at that point. It is important to take committee members through the buying phases together if at all possible. In a later chapter, we'll show you an approach for coordinating activities during committee sales.

Vendors Are Part of the Problem

Few companies are aware of or concerned about the human buying behavior we just described. They may be too focused on selling and closing deals to step back and realize that the selling process doesn't provide a positive buying experience. There are specific areas where companies steer salespeople down a path where buyers do not want to go:

- They encourage bad behavior on the part of their salespeople (e.g., encouraging them to overcome rather than address product objections, and so on).

- Despite the continuous drumbeat by sales management to "build value" throughout the sales cycle, any notion of true value is trivialized by end-of-month, end-of-quarter, or year-end pushes to discount in order to bring the deal in based on the vendor's desired close date rather than when the buyer is ready to buy.

- Many companies mistake product training for sales training. When a new product is introduced, the product management teams beats the 864 unique and robust features into the salespeople's heads, but they rarely, if ever, bother to explain why anyone would need those features or how they would actually be used in a typical business situation.

- If nonproduct sales training is offered, it often focuses on gimmicks and techniques that are designed to manipulate the buyers (have you ever heard of the "puppy dog close" or the "Columbo close"?).

- For companies that seek to "define their sales process," the focus is usually on "how do we want to sell?" rather than "how does my customer want to buy?" If you look at many sales processes that are defined in CRM applications, you'll typically see stages such as "Suspect-Prospect-Qualified-Demo-Proposal-Close." Where is the way buyers want to buy factored in?

Summary

How many mothers, when looking lovingly into the eyes of their new-born infants, ever think to themselves, "I hope you grow up to be a salesperson"? Why would our mothers, the people who probably love us in the most unconditional fashion, bristle at the idea of little Timmy or Tammy growing up to be a salesperson? We would suggest that much of the answer is derived from their own negative experiences with salespeople over the years. Given the choice of lawyer, doctor, accountant, or salesperson, which one would your mother have chosen for you?

Vendors, salespeople, and even buyers have all contributed to the view of selling as an exercise in sleight-of-hand manipulation rather than a profession. Vendors encourage and often reward bad behaviors like closing deals at quarter end. Salespeople have been guilty of the "hammer/nail" mentality. Buyers have figured out that if they are able to create the illusion of a multivendor bakeoff, they gain the greatest leverage when it comes to price negotiation.

At one point in time, this dysfunctional relationship worked to the advantage of vendors and salespeople and against buyers. The key was control of information. When buyers were compelled to interact with vendors and salespeople early in the process in order to accurately determine and define their requirements, that need for information was the leverage that the vendors and salespeople had. That was pre-Internet.

As we'll discuss in the next chapter, with the advent of the true information age that began in the early 1990s and matured about 10 years later with the IPO of Google and other online resources, the balance of power has shifted. Everything has changed. B2B buyers have begun to level the playing field when dealing with salespeople.

BUYER'S REVENGE

Imagine a police officer having to serve time in prison among inmates whom he had arrested and testified against to convict. Talk about your worst nightmare! If you give people who feel they've been wronged a chance to lash out to avenge injustices, get out of the way!

In the history of humankind, it is doubtful that there has ever been another group that approaches the sheer number of collective buyers worldwide that would savor an opportunity to even the score with salespeople and vendors who lied, misled, manipulated, extorted, overpromised, or otherwise took advantage of them. Having been victimized by poor buying experiences over time, all buyers needed to ignite a revolution was the ability to turn the tables on the salespeople.

And then, seemingly overnight, *it* happened.

It was the Internet and everything that goes with it. In a remarkably short period of time, buyers began to discover that the Internet provided a means for them to level the playing field or, better yet, gain the upper hand when dealing with salespeople. It is ironic that vendors' predictable desire to control the sales process started the revolutionary ball rolling. Without much thought, vendors jumped on the bandwagon and created Web sites that gave visitors access to as much information as, or often more information than, they ever wanted. Of course, competitors responded in marathon attempts to "one-up" the competition, and soon all products and companies were represented online.

As a result, the wardens unknowingly provided keys to the inmates. The power to control information about offerings that vendors had previously enjoyed was being given away. This started the buyer revolution without a shot being fired. As the American heavy metal band Twisted Sister famously exclaimed in its 1984 hit, "We're not gonna take it" became the rallying cry for the formerly repressed, but now newly empowered buyers. There was no turning back.

In the mid-1990s, vendor usage of the Internet started with very basic Web sites. Technology, largely because of the available speeds of

Internet connections, limited what was possible. Vendors, however, could allow 24/7 access to Web sites providing visitors with information about their companies and offerings. The Web pages describing products were "offering-intense," amounting to glorified electronic brochures complete with all types of technical specifications that would not hold the attention of executive-level B2B buyers for very long. Vendors soon realized that reduced printing costs and, even more important, version control of collateral were benefits of using this new medium.

Vendors selling commodities or relatively simple offerings were the earliest casualties of the buyer rebellion. Without fully considering the consequences of this strategy, some of these vendors decided that they could go beyond merely providing information and publish their pricing on the Web. This enabled buyers to create columns for vendors without talking to any of their salespeople—something that was unheard of just a few years earlier.

This step began the erosion of a salesperson's influence over buying decisions. It was analogous to a car dealer posting the actual prices it was willing to take on all the cars in its lot. All buyers know that the sticker price (manufacturer's suggested retail price) is merely a starting point. Getting the actual price means that you have to interface with a salesperson and arrive at a final negotiated price after a ritualistic negotiation dance . . . a dance that every buyer dreads and tries fervently to avoid. The need to interface with a seller afforded opportunities, of course, to influence buyer requirements, add features, and ultimately drive the final price higher. Dealer add-ons were a favorite because they provided fat margins.

Imagine how empowered B2B buyers felt when they realized that they were able to do two things by leveraging the Internet with vendors that provided pricing:

1. Obtain multiple bids for comparable offerings so that they could arrive at a decision without ever speaking with a salesperson.

2. Decide to buy from a particular vendor and solicit competitive bids to gain pricing leverage with Column A without having to

deal with any other salespeople. This meant that some vendors were losing transactions as Column B or C without even having their salespeople make a call! You could say that their cost of sales was reduced, but actually their cost of losing was reduced—a Pyrrhic victory for vendors, but a clear win for buyers.

Web sites began to enable enlightened buyers to engage vendors in skirmishes in a limited percentage of transactions. This proved to be the tip of the iceberg, as technologies advanced and gave buyers further capabilities to continue to reduce a seller's role in influencing their requirements. Buyers could begin to dictate to vendors how they wanted to buy. It gave buyers the control over decisions that they had craved for years.

Searching for Control

When buyers were looking for a particular B2B offering, one of the challenges in the mid-1990s was discovering the vendors that competed in the space in which they were interested. In other words, how could buyers learn which Web sites to visit and spend time on? They could try to access industry reports that gave an idea of which companies were in the space. They could ask some of their friends and colleagues for input. The net result was that compiling a list required some effort and could take a fair amount of time.

Search engines came to the rescue with a diverse range of choices from AltaVista, Yahoo!, Excite, Northern Light, Lycos, MSN, and finally Google. The latter, of course, achieved the status of being the first to truly become a household word. A buyer could now type in key words and in tenths of a second have a list of hundreds or thousands of potential Web sites to visit presented to her. This dramatically reduced the time needed and, just as important, enabled greater thoroughness in evaluating choices to include on a "short list" of vendors to be initially considered and ultimately allowed to bid. Buyers came to realize that positions in search engines were going to the highest bidders, but they had the ability to go as far down the list as they wanted.

As vendor experience with the Internet grew, visits to certain Web sites became far more effective, providing a more positive buyer experience. Vendors had migrated from electronic brochures and now offered other forms of information, such as client success stories— success stories that the vendor had, of course, cherry-picked. Rare indeed is the Web site that touts "failure stories."

Technological advances allowed the utilization of audio and video, reducing the amount of clicking and reading that was necessary. Portable Document Format (PDF) files could be easily downloaded, allowing buyers to review the material at their convenience offline (on an airplane, commuter train, or somewhere else), either by using their desktop or laptop or by printing hard copies. Webinars (or recordings of Webinars) became available as a means of assessing what offerings were relevant and what vendors were industry leaders.

All of these advances were welcomed by buyers and were helpful in making their research more efficient, but one fundamental problem remained. Based upon their ingrained distrust of salespeople, buyers were skeptical about the claims that vendors made about their offerings. They fully expected that sellers and vendors would overstate (hype) the capabilities they offered, and they took the sellers' claims with a grain of salt. While there was a tremendous volume of data available on the Internet, the vast majority was being "pushed" to buyers. What we mean by that is each vendor exerted complete control over what buyers were able to learn about its company and its offerings. Would your grades in high school have been better if you had been able to fill out your own report card?

Everyone Is a Publisher

Users soon discovered that the Internet was a freely accessible two-way street. It wasn't only corporations that could create Web sites.

Anyone could do so, and at virtually no cost. But why would, say, an individual want to do so?

One answer was the emergence of blogs. According to the online encyclopedia Wikipedia, "A blog (a contraction of the term 'Web log') is a Web site, usually maintained by an individual with regular entries of commentary, descriptions of events, or other material such as graphics or video." Personal and business blogging became popular and further eroded a vendor's ability to project the image it wanted to project to buyers and thereby influence their perceptions.

There is an oft-quoted statistic that a happy customer will tell 4 people about his experience, while an unhappy customer will tell 13. With blogs, customers could easily and instantly share their perceptions with millions of readers who found the blog in a search return. And, given the nature of how search engines work, the Web page with the user's opinion could achieve permanent residency on the Internet. The implications of this ability for anyone to shape opinions about a company and its offerings were, and are, significant.

Blogging became word of mouth on steroids. For the first time, raw, unedited perspectives and opinions about offerings, vendors, quality of offerings, ease of use, service, support, and other such factors became available to anyone who wanted to read them. There was the ability for some electronic interchange on specific areas, with multiple people being able to participate. Having said that, there were some shortcomings that limited the effectiveness of blogs.

Buyers, having been burned over the years, soon came to realize that some bloggers were more "legitimate" than others. While certainly unethical, it was not beyond the realm of possibility for salespeople or vendors to cut and paste success stories from their Web sites and post self-serving glowing testimonials on blogs. Alas, buyers have long honed their skills at detecting when they are being manipulated, so generally these attempts failed. Just as citizens have to watch, listen, and read various news outlets and determine for themselves what the facts are, the same is true for those who conduct Internet research.

What emerged was an ever-growing number of credible blogs that were (apparently) independent and transparent. The ability for followers of these blogs to add comments on each blog post created rich communities of people united by a common interest or topic. Sure, an unscrupulous seller could publish a self-serving post about how great her products were, but the blog would either earn no following or receive strong contrarian comments, if deserved. And once comments were made, they were essentially permanent, appearing in search results anytime someone typed in the right phrase or word.

Based upon this inherent distrust, negative comments on blogs were more readily perceived and accepted as being true. Another shortcoming was that visitors to blogs most often did not know the bloggers, thereby reducing the impact of the information that they shared. Even assuming that it wasn't a salesperson or vendor that was blogging, how much faith could a visitor place in the positive opinion of someone he neither knew nor trusted?

Social Networking

Social networking isn't new. It's been around for a long time in a local, community, or organizational setting. What is new is online social networking, which combines the candor of blogs with the ability to solicit opinions from a network of buyers that are known and trusted. Now users can network not only with people locally but around the world just by searching on common interests in social networking applications such as LinkedIn, MySpace, Facebook, Twitter, or Jigsaw.

The buyer's dream come true became a potential nightmare for vendors. It was no longer good enough to pay lip service to the fact that you were "customer-centric." Companies now had to build a culture to deliver on that promise. For the first time, vendors began to reap what they sowed, as unfiltered opinions that ran the gamut from glowing to scathing came directly from trusted buyers. Regardless of where the input fell on the scale from good to bad, it had equal credibility. And it was largely believable.

Case Study: Using Social Networking to Select a Vendor

We thought an example of leveraging social networking would be helpful for fully appreciating how this is changing buying behavior and habits. In 2008, CustomerCentric Selling® decided to hire an adult learning specialist for a project. Rather than using a search engine and then visiting multiple Web sites where every consulting group was trying to put its best foot forward, we took a different approach. We described our situation, the scope of the engagement, and the type of consultant we were looking for and electronically polled our social networks of trusted people for suggestions and recommendations. We used tools such as LinkedIn and searched public profiles of candidates who might meet our criteria and had the experience we were looking for. We cross-referenced their backgrounds with other searches to verify the credibility of their claims, all without speaking to any of them.

Within a week, three candidates emerged who seemed to have the background and skills that we required. We had developed our short list of vendors without talking to any of the consultants. Between the references from our network and the descriptions on the consultants' Web sites, one candidate appeared to be the best choice. That consultant was called and handled our questions in a professional manner. We asked for three references for work that was done for engagements similar in scope to ours. The references checked out, and within two weeks, we had finalized an agreement.

We, the buyer, were in complete control the entire time. The consultants who weren't selected, those who lost, never even knew that they were in the game. They would have been contacted if our interaction with the first vendor hadn't gone well. In our case, we determined that it didn't make sense to "run a beauty contest" by inviting the others to bid in order to get quotes. Our rationale was that consulting rates didn't vary greatly, and time was of the essence.

Imagine the implications for B2B vendors today. Prospects can visit your Web site, gain insight into your offerings and reputation by leveraging media including social networking, and even get an idea of how you price your offerings. At that point, the following things can happen:

- You don't make the short list based upon the buyer's perception of your offering, reputation, pricing, support, or other factors.

- You are invited to compete, but there is a clear "Column A" that owns the requirements list. Unless your seller can alter the list of the buyer's needs, you are merely being brought in for pricing leverage with the vendor of choice.

- You are invited to compete along with some other competitors, and there is no favored vendor.

It is now commonplace for potential buyers to share issues that they are facing and seek guidance online from others who have faced and solved these problems. They electronically search Web resources and poll their trusted communities for input about specific companies and their offerings. In doing so, they receive firsthand input from buyers relating their buying experience with the salesperson, the functionality of the offering, support, reliability, ease of use, and so on. When salespeople are finally contacted, buyers are knowledgeable about their requirements and the available offerings from several vendors. The chances that they will be manipulated or oversold are dramatically reduced. Knowledge is power. It has shifted into the hands of savvy buyers. This trend is gaining momentum and fast becoming the norm.

As you can see, the progression of developments has steadily reduced the ability of both salespeople and vendors to influence buyers' requirements and decisions. B2B buyers are now able to refer to the conceptual equivalent of a *Consumer Reports* and get transparent opinions about things that they are interested in buying from trusted sources that have no financial stake in the final decision. Buyers also have a stake in both gleaning and providing input.

While the research on buying curves and phases remains valid, the sequencing of the seller's involvement means that initial seller contacts with buyers are different from what they were pre-Internet. Most salespeople are ill prepared to make an initial call on a knowledgeable buyer. Failing to align with these buyers can compromise the buying experience. We'd now like to apply the findings on buying curves to the new way buyers buy. We refer to this as "empowered buying" or "empowered buyers." The major takeaway for you is an awareness of how to better align with this new type of buyer.

Buying: Ten Years Later

The major difference between now and the middle to late 1990s is that empowered buyers are now able to define their requirements by utilizing electronic means and, most important, without speaking with salespeople. Since salespeople are being denied the luxury of participating during Phase 1, there isn't necessarily any "Column A" salesperson or vendor. The buyer requirements are an aggregate of all the research and input the buyer has analyzed. The buyer requirements chart that you saw in Chapter 1 now changes to that shown in Figure 2-1.

The reality today is that the buying experience for a particular vendor begins when a potential buyer accesses that company's Web site or signs on to a Webinar that it is hosting. The "requirements" list, created before talking with a salesperson, represents the aggregate of visiting multiple vendor Web sites, looking at blogs, and engaging in social networking. The buyer can readily learn a ballpark figure for what an offering will cost. This means that the buyer has entered Phase 2 of the buying cycle through self-service and is now starting to evaluate vendors to determine which one represents the best buying decision.

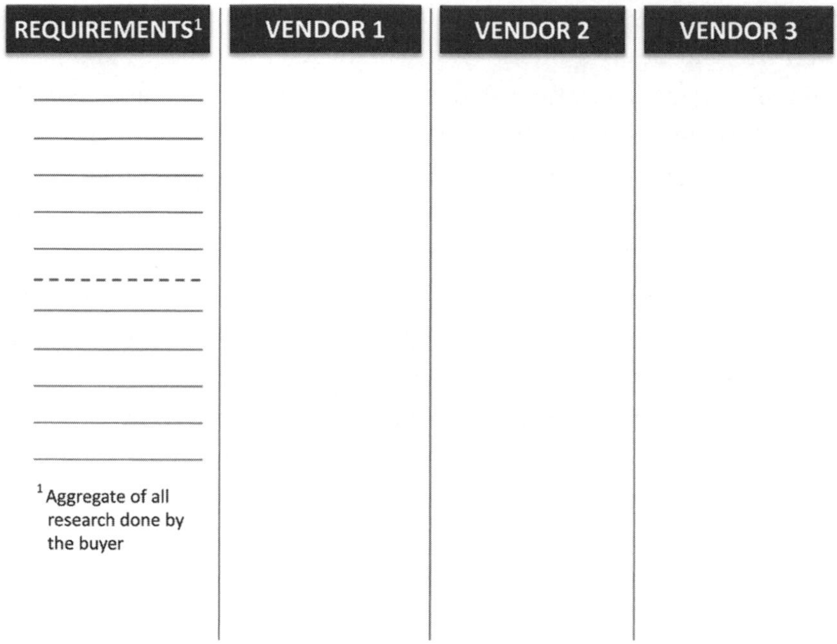

REQUIREMENTS[1]	VENDOR 1	VENDOR 2	VENDOR 3

[1] Aggregate of all research done by the buyer

Figure 2-1

How the Empowered Buyer Responds to Cold Calls

Empowered buying provides a plausible explanation for the number of articles and books that are declaring either the death or the diminishing effectiveness of cold calling. Assume for a minute that you receive a compelling voice mail from a salesperson that raised a business issue that you hadn't been considering, but that you become interested in addressing. Would you would call the salesperson (someone you don't know) right back? Or would you go online and do a quick search to see what you could find out? If you did, where would that search take you?

An empowered buyer might begin by looking at the company's Web site and product offerings. It would be easy to learn about the credibility (size, scope, and so on) of the company and get a sense of what the company stood for. The downside is that all of the information being looked at is controlled by the vendor and therefore likely to be biased.

While some buyers may then call the salesperson back, many empowered buyers would let their fingers do the walking. A point and a click would take them to a search result listing competitive offerings, reviews of the company, and forums or blogs discussing different topics. Given that the seller's voice mail awakened a need in the buyer, the empowered buyer may now be inspired to engage others online in conversations regarding how they had approached solving common problems. At some point, the empowered buyer will feel that she has enough information and, if motivated to do so, will initiate contact—but not necessarily with the salesperson whose cold call ignited the interest. She may start with the solution that emerged as most promising as a result of the online counsel that she received and trusted. She may or may not contact the seller that deserves credit for initiating the buying cycle.

Aligning with Buying Phases

Life is not fair. If you choose not to call the seller whose voice mail first aroused your interest, this is an example of sales imitating life. In 1990, you would have returned the call, and the seller could start to develop your needs in Phase 1 with a bias toward his offering. Today, a seller who is contacted after research has been completed will be talking with a buyer who is already in Phase 2.

For complex offerings, even though a buyer is in Phase 2, there will almost certainly be some requirements that either are on the list and don't belong there or that should be on it but are missing. This is a result of the buyer's not having had a thorough discussion with a competent seller to understand her current situation and determine the specific capabilities needed to improve her business results. Above and beyond the offering itself, there may be implementation issues and professional services that will be necessary to address them. This would entail a separate need development effort to create the implementation solution.

Returning to the buyer who has researched offerings, the real challenge is for salespeople who have been trained and therefore are most familiar with encountering buyers who are in Phase 1. Traditional selling techniques have been designed and are most effective with buyers who do not understand their requirements. As you can see, the buyer (in Phase 2) and seller (acting as though the buyer is in Phase 1) are out of alignment. This highlights one of the most common problems with sales calls that don't go well.

Trying to do Phase 1 selling with knowledgeable buyers can begin a premature downward spiral. Early in an interaction, if a seller tries to add requirements that are not on the list (sell), the buyer will feel that he is being manipulated. In order to align with a buyer who has done extensive research, the first questions should relate to interest qualification: finding out what the buyer feels his requirements are and establishing competence in the mind of the buyer. It will also be helpful to the buyer if the business drivers behind the potential purchase are uncovered. As each goal is uncovered, continue interest qualification by learning what requirements relate to achieving the stated goal.

If interest qualification is successfully completed by taking these steps, the buyer will be willing to allow a salesperson to take him back into Phase 1 to further develop and refine the requirements list. The buyer is not a blank canvas, but the seller can develop strong credibility by uncovering additional requirements and/or by having the buyer realize that some of the requirements on the original list either are unnecessary or won't work in his environment. This ideally would be done by asking questions rather than by telling the buyer what he needs. Asking questions enables the buyer to draw his own conclusions. A seller that can get this far during the initial contacts stands a good chance of becoming Column A. It is critical for a seller to allow the buyer to share the opinions that he has formed as a result of the research that he's done.

This sequence also indicates why internally developed RFPs (requests for proposal), or more likely RFIs (requests for information), are so difficult to win if vendors are unable to influence the requirements by understanding the buyer's needs. You receive what amounts to an organizational list of Phase 2 requirements and are asked (actually told) to explain how your offering meets each requirement and what the total associated costs are. There is no selling to be done unless you can have meaningful conversations with some of the key players involved in the buying decision. Buyer paranoia about sellers manipulating them causes them to issue a "half-baked" requirements list.

We hope you would agree that companies that have implemented and are using customer relationship management (CRM) systems institutionalize misalignment with buyers if

- Their milestones were designed without taking the buying process into account.

- Their sales milestones are designed for a traditional sale where sellers participate in developing buyer needs in Phase 1.

- They adopt the stereotypical definition of selling as convincing, persuading, overcoming objections, and so on. This approach will offend a buyer who has done her homework.

- They train their salespeople in traditional sales techniques.

The result for such salespeople in initial calls will be tension between the buyer and the seller and ultimately a poor buying experience. After such calls, it should be no surprise that the vendors won't make the short list (unless they are needed for pricing leverage with Column A).

Summary

Awareness is the first step in taking corrective action. Companies that understand the new way in which people are evaluating and acquiring B2B offerings have a tremendous opportunity to make the way their salespeople sell (empower buyers to buy) a sustainable competitive advantage. It isn't an easy journey, but in Part 3 of the book, we'll lay out an approach for getting there.

Perhaps you'll agree that traditional B2B selling was never really in favor. Rather, it was tolerated because there was no viable alternative for making buying decisions. As summarized in the previous chapter, B2B sellers were stereotyped based upon early negative experiences with B2C sellers. Even without that stereotype, the manner in which vendors and their salespeople defined selling set the stage for confrontations with buyers that would have caused the same conclusions about sellers to be reached.

Frustrated by the continuing onslaught of manipulation by sellers, buyers finally began to see alternatives. Some buyer reactions may have been inspired by exposure to B2C companies that improved the customer's buying experience by completely eliminating salespeople—an example of such a B2C company is Amazon.com. While this is not possible for complex offerings, a seller's influence on buyer requirements can be greatly reduced. Toward that end, today's buyer wants to go into the buying process as far as possible before having any contact with salespeople. Buying experiences that begin electronically are becoming the rule, and that trend will continue. In this environment, traditional selling approaches that were annoying in 1990 have now become obnoxious to informed buyers. Buyers are not going to take it anymore and will talk to vendors with their corporate checkbooks.

The three phases of buying cycles provide a framework that allows sellers to better understand the decision-making process. It describes human buying behavior that will evolve slowly over time. As we've pointed out, the Internet has changed the timing and nature of the first interaction that sellers have with buyers.

To describe how to influence the B2B buying experience, a more in-depth view of how buying has changed is necessary. In Part 2, we will describe how buyers have leveraged the Internet during five stages of buying cycles:

- Stage 1: Awareness and urgency

- Stage 2: Research

- Stage 3: Preference

- Stage 4: Reassurance

- Stage 5: Risk—the go/no-go buying decision

More important, we'll offer our views about how selling at the tactical marketing, salesperson, and enterprise levels has to change to align with the new buying behavior. While this is challenging, tremendous benefits will accrue to those who can facilitate positive buying experiences.

PART 2

The Five Stages of the B2B Buying Cycle

STAGE 1: AWARENESS AND URGENCY–INITIATING THE BUYING CYCLE

We all know that eating healthy foods, maintaining a reasonable weight, and exercising at least three times a week are desirable habits. Yet over time, we consume supersized fast-food meals, the readings on the scale steadily creep higher, and the treadmill in the basement gathers dust. People have busy lives and are being pulled in multiple directions simultaneously. We can handle only a finite number of issues at any given time. Good health is taken for granted, meaning that diet, weight, and level of exercise can take a backseat to the general activities and pressures of our personal and business lives. Unlike those who live to stay in shape, most of us aren't focused on the changes in either our metabolism or our physique over time. Things that are perceived to be status quo are not questioned unless something causes us to consider or question them.

A wake-up call can quickly bring diet, weight, and exercise to the forefront. The ways in which you become aware that these areas require attention vary both in urgency and in effectiveness. Your spouse, a relative, or a friend tells you that you need to go on a diet. You see an article or an ad on the Internet and realize that you look more like the before than like the after picture. A major wardrobe investment looms because everything in your closet except for a recently purchased Hawaiian luau shirt is too small. A doctor informs you after a physical that your lifestyle is putting you at risk for major health issues. You suffer a health scare.

The most effective ways to heighten awareness about health are those that are self-realized or that arise from concern expressed by a trusted medical professional. Just as people like to buy rather than be sold, we don't like to be told what we need to do by people who we feel are meddling in our affairs. Even though the person offering it may be right and well intentioned, unsolicited advice is rejected far more often than it is taken to heart.

In our personal lives, the first step in bringing about change is awareness that a goal (desire to lose weight) or a problem (I'm overweight) exists. Next comes determining whether there is an adequate sense of urgency to motivate you to address the issue being considered. If there is, you will analyze the underlying factors causing your condition, explore ways to address them, and determine what you feel are the best courses of action to lose weight. Awareness of a problem or need is where it all starts. The catalysts that drive change, however, are motivation and a sense of urgency.

The litmus test for your sense of urgency at this point is questioning whether the sacrifices (giving up foods you like; eating less) and effort (exercising on a regular basis) required will be more than offset by the perceived benefits of being more fit and healthy. If you decide to go ahead, sustaining your efforts without slipping back into old habits requires an ongoing sense of urgency and motivation. If you decide that losing weight isn't worth the sacrifices you are making, it becomes the latest initiative added to your list of failed New Year's resolutions. You'll wait for another wake-up call. Hopefully it will be one that is not too severe.

Not All Memory Can Be Expanded

The human mind can be compared to a computer. Both have finite amounts of usable memory. Computer memory can sometimes be expanded, but even then only to a degree. It too is finite.

Researchers have found that, on average, people have 7 + /- 2 foreground slots available for actively considering issues. Stated another way, people on average can juggle 5 to 9 things in their minds at any given time. This may be the reason that we sometimes make "to do" lists at the end or beginning of the business day. When we write items down, we don't have to tie up slots trying to remember them, freeing us up to think about other things.

It would be a mistake to assume that the number of slots a person has is proportional to that person's intelligence. Over the years, some of the most brilliant people we've encountered have had one enormous slot (or could allocate multiple slots to a single issue). When such people wrestle with a problem, they are consumed to the point where they can deal with little else. They arrive at work with two different shoes on. Personal hygiene takes a backseat while they brainstorm. Given enough time, they will figure out solutions to problems that few people are capable of resolving. Having fewer slots enables some brilliant people to be "single-minded" in solving issues.

If all of your slots are full and a new issue is going to be entertained, it must be perceived as being more important than the least important issue that is currently occupying one of your slots. If it is, the least important issue will be pushed off the list, making room for the new one. This conceptually describes an environment in which there is *continuous competition for mind share.* Slots are allocated based upon the relative importance or sense of urgency that each issue carries with it. Because of the finite number of slots we have, it would be abnormal behavior for us to keep slots allocated to issues that we consider to be either beyond our control or unsolvable (worrying if the weather will be nice next week, worrying about the economy, and so on). You may consider such issues briefly, but unless you are depressed or mentally ill, you won't obsess over them. They'll occupy slots for small slices of time and then be discarded in favor of issues that can be resolved.

Marketing versus Sales

Throughout this book, we will use often the terms *seller* and *vendor.* Sometimes we'll be more specific and discuss the role of the *salesperson* or the *marketer.* For the purposes of this book, they really all mean the same thing, as there are only two sides of buying decisions: buyer and seller. In the same way that we have offered a new definition of selling, we'll propose a different way to view lead generation and nurturing in Part 3.

In our view, marketing and selling exist along a single continuum designed to connect a company (the vendor) with buyers and customers. The most fundamental goal of marketing is to reduce the cost of selling; otherwise, why not just have every company abandon marketing and put a million sales reps on the street? Marketing can employ tactics that increase reach at a much more favorable cost than the ridiculous notion of hiring a million salespeople.

The skill sets and mindsets of marketing and sales "types" are quite different. Over time, this has caused divergence and friction between these two related but separate functions. Marketing is viewed as more creative, abstract, and strategic, while sales is viewed as more aggressive, mercenary, and tactical. Naturally, these differences attract people with different personality traits to marketing and sales. With reference to our evolutionary ascent, some view marketing as farmers and sales as hunters. Metaphorically, they share the common objective of providing food to eat (generating revenue).

Marketing and sales may exist along the same customer acquisition continuum, but they haven't been structured that way. Organizationally, companies began to separate sales from marketing, and soon there was both a VP of sales and a VP of marketing. There was little sense in being a VP if you didn't have an organization, so further fractionalization and polarization was often the result. On the marketing side, along came functions such as channel marketing, event marketing, marketing communications, product marketing, and so on. Each had its head, its staff, its admins (administrative support), and its own budget.

On the sales side, the need arose for geographic sales, vertical market sales, major account sales, product sales, inside sales, and so on. To make matters more confusing, the role of "field marketing" was added to the sales side, and no one could agree on whether "inside sales" belonged with marketing (lead generation) or with sales (territory coverage)!

This mindset created silos, particularly within U.S. companies, and soon a glaring disconnect emerged between sales and marketing. Forget about being on the same page; these organizations weren't even reading the same book! In our experience, European companies often employed "country managers" who had a more holistic perspective, so the problems associated with silos weren't quite as bad. For the most part, it was agreed (ubiquitously and without vote) that the intersection of sales and marketing for B2B companies would be at the "lead handoff."

Marketing's focus in B2B settings became to generate leads. Sales's role became, as it always had been, to close them. It is noteworthy that many salespeople, partly as a result of distrusting marketing's likelihood of success, continued their own prospecting/lead generation. Sales prospecting focuses on specific target opportunities where short-term decisions will be made or where relationship building is crucial. This is largely due to the fact that salespeople are compensated and measured on short-term results, such as this quarter's quota. Marketing tends to cast a broader net in an attempt to "get a bite" from prospects that represent qualified opportunities or that may be developed over time.

The Sales Benchmark Index, in a 2008 report cosponsored by CustomerCentric Selling®, surveyed world-class sales organizations (WCSOs) in an effort to find best practices that yielded superior results. Part of that report found that companies that performed at world-class levels relied more heavily on centralized lead generation than other organizations. The survey concluded that formal lead-generation programs that had to be cost-justified were more effective than ad hoc attempts at business development by individual salespeople.

Within WCSOs, the number of leads generated by territory salespeople was 47 percent lower than the norm. The report indicated that reduced business development efforts allowed salespeople more time to focus on moving opportunities that were already in the pipeline along, and this ultimately resulted in higher close rates.

Other than at the handoff point of a lead, there is often minimal constructive communication between marketing and sales in most corporations. Once leads are passed to sales, it's a common cry of marketing that it never knows what happens to them. (How many organizations formally define and frequently update what constitutes a lead?) When challenged, salespeople counter that the leads from marketing are of poor quality, and that they need more high-quality leads if they are to make their numbers. The blame cycle continues.

So, what is a seller to do in an effort to create awareness on the part of the buyer? Let's examine the predictable human behavior that buyers exhibit to provide a landscape of how buying cycles can be initiated.

Getting Inside the Buyer's Head

Technology has exponentially increased the volume of information we are exposed to in our lives. Pre-Internet times, when printed media, radio, and television bombarded us primarily during our leisure hours, are now distant memories of a simpler era. The Internet exposes us to an overwhelming volume of messages during the workday and the leisure time we spend online. It is impossible to entertain everything that is being pushed at us. Slot management is the way we have learned to filter and cope with the relentless flood of attempts to gain our interest.

Buyers can be categorized based upon their level of need. *Active* needs are issues that buyers are actively trying to address (slots are allocated). *Latent* needs, on the other hand, are potential needs that buyers aren't focusing on (no slots are allocated). The illustration in Figure 3-1 shows how you can look at your potential market at specific sales territory, regional, or global levels. First, choose an offering and then think, as of this moment, what percentage of the companies in your total market are actively looking for your offering (whether it be yours or those of your competitors), meaning that they are actively evaluating, have budget allocated, and will be making a buying decision within the time frame of an average sales cycle. Most people find that this is a relatively small percentage (10 percent or less). Vendors with a disruptive offering may find that the number of people actively looking approaches 0 percent.

In looking at marketing's pipeline as it relates to leads, there are latent and active needs, but a third category is necessary to describe a large number of potential buyers that fall somewhere in between. We'll label this group as "curious." By this we mean that your offer-

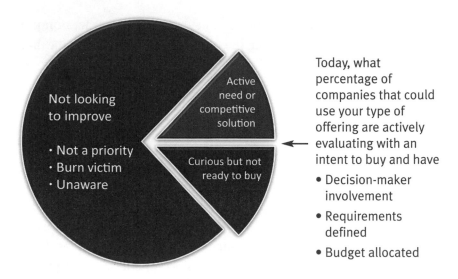

Today, what percentage of companies that could use your type of offering are actively evaluating with an intent to buy and have

- Decision-maker involvement
- Requirements defined
- Budget allocated

Figure 3-1

ing has piqued their curiosity, but they aren't ready for serious evaluation to determine if they should buy. This group represents the vast majority of prospects in the marketing pipeline.

We've heard vendors make comments that caused us to create this category, such as: "We have about a four-month sales cycle once buyers are ready to do a serious evaluation, but sometimes it can take two years for them to get to that point." We'll revisit this group later, which generally is the bubble on the bell curve, but first we want to focus on the buyers that have a latent need and provide suggested approaches to migrate them to active need.

Consider companies that aren't looking. The majority of them are facing the same issues as the companies that are already looking. There are three primary reasons why companies that have issues are not actively trying to address them:

1. They don't consider the issue to be a priority. They have other things on their plates that they perceive as being more important (no memory slots are allocated).

2. They tried to address the issue one or more times in the past, with mixed or poor results, and can't justify another attempt. We refer to such buyers as burn victims. Yet another failed attempt could be a career-limiting move. If a slot is allocated, the buyer remembers past failures, realizes that the issue may not be addressable, and reallocates the slot to another matter.

3. The buyer is unaware that there is a way to address the issue.

This metaphor of gaining mind share and allocating slots provides a foundation for imagining the challenges that vendors have in proactively attempting to start buying cycles. Buyers with latent needs represent the greatest potential for your offerings by a 9:1 margin if only 10 percent of your market has active needs.

It may surprise you to realize that most B2B executive-level buyers do not have needs for your offerings. Rather, they have needs that can be addressed through the use of your offerings. This is a critical distinction that many sellers never "get." As legendary Harvard Business School marketing professor Theodore Levitt used to tell his students, "People don't want to buy a quarter-inch drill. They want a quarter-inch hole!" In today's world of feature/benefit-laden vocabulary, it seems that virtually every marketing and sales professional either missed the professor's class or has never internalized his quote. Vendors who are focused on their offerings are more inward- than outward-looking. At "C level," or the executive level, offering-intense attempts to generate interest fall on deaf ears. The focus at that level is all about improving business results.

The ability to initiate buying cycles and become Column A on a regular basis is possible only at the executive level. These buyers lack the time and patience to be nurtured. If they realize that there is an offering that can enable improved business results, they will start a buying cycle and often delegate the detailed evaluation to lower levels within their organizations. Buying cycles begun this way tend to go more quickly and have a lower probability of ending in "no decision."

To get a better sense of how to create awareness, it may be helpful to ask yourself a simple question: what bad things happen to business results for buyers with a particular title (CEO, VP Sales, and so on) in a particular vertical (health care, financial services, and so on) or geographic (e.g., North America or Europe) market because they aren't using your offering? The answers can be embedded in a message crafted in such a way as to kill two birds with one stone. It can both generate awareness and increase the urgency to act by illustrating the financial impact if the potential buyer does nothing.

This approach also aligns with Phase 1 of the buying curves. A buying cycle begins when a memory slot is allocated to a business issue. At that moment, the buyers' major concerns are their needs and the price of the offering. As you may remember, the importance of price declines over time provided the buyer recognizes potential value in the offering that he is considering. Delaying pricing discussions is not only necessary when using electronic media (pricing can't be provided until requirements are known), but also *desirable for the seller* until additional value can be perceived in the buyer's mind.

Human nature is such that people place a higher value on potential losses than on gains. For that reason, in initiating buying cycles, our suggestion is to lead with problems rather than goals. In the B2C example, this would be being overweight (problem) versus wanting to be thinner (goal). To gain mind share for a weight-loss program, an image of an overweight person will be more effective than one of someone who is fit. Once a need goes from latent to active, it is assigned a slot. It will end in one of two ways:

• The buyer takes action and buys from a vendor.

• The buyer again rationalizes that addressing the issue is too complicated, too expensive, no longer a priority, and so on.

It's All in Their Mind

Gaining mind share is how we define the beginning of B2B buying cycles. For disruptive offerings or unplanned purchases, the challenge is to make people aware that the offerings exist and have them recognize potential problems that can be addressed by using the offerings. As an example of a disruptive offering, imagine that your company develops a centralized on-demand printing offering that clients could use to save millions of dollars in wasted printing and transportation costs . . . if only they knew about it.

When you introduce this product to them, they may be intrigued and act, but they had not previously allocated budget for it or set up a decision committee because they didn't know that such an item was even available. Budget, therefore, must be made available, and to make the sale happen, the salesperson must have access to a level (C level) that can approve a large investment, often by reallocating money by canceling previously funded projects. This is a disruptive sale.

A mistake that we've seen vendors of disruptive technologies make has been to feel that their salespeople have to educate people on their new offerings. The people who would be most interested in and willing to learn about the quarter-inch drill are relatively low in the organization and can't approve significant unbudgeted expenses. Initiating interest at higher levels about usage (the quarter-inch hole) will qualify prospects sooner and facilitate a top-down rather than a bottom-up approach. High-level executives will not waste their time evaluating offerings that they don't see potential value in using.

For continuous improvement or replacement offerings, the approach is to have buyers realize the advantages of the new version over older offerings and the potential benefits of using it. A good example of a continuous improvement offering would be an upgrade to a company's telephone system. This may have been something that the company knew in advance had to be done and had budgeted/planned accordingly, or an enterprising salesperson or vendor may have helped the company realize the shortcomings of its installed phone system.

Whether an offering is categorized as being disruptive or continuous improvement, targeting people at high levels offers three significant advantages. First, at executive levels, the number of issues that buyers face decreases in number, but increases in importance. Second, calling at high levels means that buyers can find budget for expenditures that hadn't been planned for. Finally, generating interest at higher levels generally means shorter buying cycles. This is critical if leads are going to result in sales that enable sellers to achieve this year's quota.

Curious Buyers: Nuke or Nurture Them?

While we're on the subject of quota pressure, the largest number of potential buyers falls into the group that is curious, yet not ready to actively begin the buying cycle. As we stereotyped sellers as hunters, unless a large opportunity was at this stage, nurturing would not be the normal course of action. The seller would move on to find another prospect who was interested in making a decision in the short term. Generally speaking, salespeople make poor nurturers of opportunities, and their compensation doesn't encourage this behavior. For that reason, marketing often assumes the role of nurturing curious buyers in hopes that if and when they are ready to begin a buying cycle, they will contact the vendor that offered the best experience in providing information as needed. This nurturing period enables a vendor to earn trust and be helpful to the buyer, laying the foundation for earning trusted-advisor status.

Just as salespeople have personality traits that buyers judge them on, buyers who are curious will also make judgments about companies based upon the way they are treated. It should be okay for people to want to kick the tires without buying. Vendors that provide industry facts and trends, newsletters, results that other customers have achieved, invitations to Webinars, and other such information without blatant attempts to do any selling will be viewed more favorably as being helpful rather than pushing buyers.

We are or soon will be at a point where the majority of B2B buying experiences begin without human contact. For that reason, we'd like to introduce the concept of providing information to curious buyers to accomplish three things:

• Gain mind share

• Initiate buying cycles

• Earn the status of being viewed as a vendor that will be contacted when the buyer is ready to start a buying cycle

Part of this buyer experience is deciding how you would like your company to be perceived by buyers in the very early stages of awareness. Once you decide on the conclusions that you want buyers to draw, the challenging step is leveraging technology to help them migrate from curious to active need at the desired pace. The least expensive (and potentially most flexible) way to accomplish this is by leveraging the Internet.

Creating Awareness Has Evolved

Considering the number of available mind slots a buyer has, and given the organizational dynamics of sales and marketing departments, how is a selling organization to create awareness with a buyer? Years ago, marketing would use some form of broad-reach advertising to create awareness, using either print ads, billboards, TV, radio, sponsorships, or some combination thereof. Awareness was important to make it easier for the salesperson to gain entry, and advertising was touted by publishers as a way to establish credibility, as the brilliant ad from McGraw-Hill in Figure 3-2 made clear way back in 1958. Creating awareness before the sales process begins makes as much sense now as it did 50 years ago.

Figure 3-2 *McGraw-Hill Ad*
Source: © The McGraw-Hill Companies, Inc. Reprinted with permission of the McGraw-Hill Companies, Inc.

Technological advances in relational database development with demographic and psychographic data points enabled marketers to create databases and deliver targeted messages. This led to strong growth in direct marketing in the 1980s and 1990s, but the goal remained to create interest and drive a response, just as it was with broad advertising. The exception, of course, is advertising that is focused on image and brand development, which generally does not employ a call to action.

As the Internet took hold, marketers feverishly sought new ways to reach their target audiences and gain mind share. E-mail replaced direct mail, but, alas, the same old habits were used. Now, instead of a physical mailbox being full of "junk," a virtual inbox was full of "junk." Buyers, seeking control over their right to privacy, screamed for ways to filter out unsolicited inquiries, and a whole new industry was born. This is an instance of marketing emulating sales behavior that buyers deeply resented.

Many organizations recognized the seriousness of the error in "spamming" (using e-mail to send unsolicited bulk messages) and developed "opt-in" lists, but this was a small minority for many years. Lists are generally purchased from somewhere, and we can promise you that even the opt-in lists that are purchased include people who either don't want unsolicited e-mail or have provided a junk e-mail address.

Vendors have made and will continue to make investments in technology that enables them to reduce their cost while increasing their reach to their target audiences. Look back at messaging in the mid-1990s, then look at some current messages. It doesn't appear that the upgrade in technology has been matched by an upgrade in the quality of the messages being used to gain buyers' interest. If anything, the lower cost of distribution has taken the focus away from spending time to develop more relevant messages that will resonate with potential buyers. As sellers have been stereotyped for past behavior, buyers soon begin to think that what sellers see as promising new ways to reach an audience are more of a nuisance than an effective way to communicate ideas.

Some approaches used in electronic media mirrored those used by the stereotypical salespeople we discussed in Chapter 1. Buyers responded in similar ways. Executives have admins (gatekeepers) to limit access by salespeople who call in. Unless the seller has something potentially relevant to discuss, he or she will be denied access. Spam filters are the electronic equivalent.

Salespeople generally probe with qualifying questions before they've earned the right to ask them. This makes buyers uncomfortable, and they feel pressured. Imagine how a curious buyer will respond to premature efforts to qualify her using today's technology. How many Web site visits end as soon as buyers are asked to provide their name, company, title, e-mail address, and so on?

Despite the fact that the marketing staff is responsible for using technology for lead generation, its members unknowingly carry baggage from their exposure to selling approaches. As soon as electronic behavior mimics what is perceived to be stereotypical selling behavior, customers' defenses are invoked and receptivity starts to wane. Many vendor behaviors using the Internet could be perceived by buyers as attempts to regain the control that was ceded when information was made available to everyone on demand. An example would be asking for contact information too soon during a Web site visit as a prerequisite for sending a PDF file of a white paper the buyer would like to see. In these circumstances, prospects are normally quite happy to jump to a competing Web site that is less intrusive and more helpful.

Often we get caught up in the "next new thing," only to realize that it wasn't really new at all. With the Internet, few marketers varied from their old approaches when utilizing different tools. Here are some examples of what amounted to a "search and replace" strategy:

Old Term	New Term
Direct mail	E-mail
Seminars	Webinars
Live trade shows	Virtual trade shows
Print ads	Banner ads
In-person networking	Virtual networking

Business response cards	Landing pages
TV commercials	YouTube videos
Broadcast radio ads	Podcasts/satellite radio

And so history repeats itself, as it normally does. Applying a heavy dose of cologne is a poor substitute for taking a shower. It is unfortunate that new vehicles convey the same old messages. Faced with the overwhelming deluge of messages that are being pushed to them on a daily basis, buyers started tuning out long ago. For countless TV and radio channels, publications, podcasts, blogs, ads, direct mail, e-mail, conferences, and events, prospective buyers see them and make snap decisions to either discard the message from their memory (almost always) or, on rare occasions, assign it a memory slot. Our job as sellers is to develop messages that enable buyers to connect our offerings with their available or occupied memory slots, and compel them to heighten their urgency. We will discuss effective messaging much more in Chapter 9, "Getting Product Marketing Right." For now, let's discuss what an organization can do to enable its message to be at the right place at the right time.

Message Control—Aligning with Buyers

In the early days, marketing's job was to create awareness of a company's products by using advertising, public relations, events, and direct marketing. Today, with credit to former president George H. W. Bush, there seem to be a thousand points of light—at least—that buyers can turn their attention to for information.

Just as salespeople can enjoy a competitive advantage by the way they sell, the same is true with attempting to gain awareness and instill a sense of urgency. Whether you are in sales or in marketing, why not step back and spend some time to determine the following for each of your offerings?

- What titles within an organization would be involved in making a buying decision?

- For each title, what business issues that can be addressed by our offering are important?

- How can we focus our sales and marketing efforts on these issues?

- What media are most effective in reaching our targeted titles?

Figure 3-3 *CustomerCentric Messaging Matrix*

	Corp. Marketing Audience	Compliance
Common Job Titles	• Marketing Communications Manager • Product Marketing Manager • Director of Marketing • Marketing Manager	• Security Officer • Director of Compliance • Chief Compliance Officer • CFO
Main Concerns	• Mail response rates • Closed loop accesibility • Speed of mail receipt • Program success • Customer experience	• Regulatory compliance • Proof of mailing • Speed • Accuracy • Security
Primary Vendor Advantage	• **Control and assurance** – Built for today's CRM needs	• **Proof** – Visual proof that the piece was mailed and on time
Secondary Advantage	**Speed**	**Speed**

One way to visualize this approach is through a tool that we refer to as a CustomerCentric Messaging Matrix®. This tool allows a marketer or seller to visualize each group that it wants to target, the titles represented in each group, the main concerns that each group faces, and the primary advantage the vendor's products offer to help address those concerns.

The matrix is shown in Figure 3-3.

Figure 3-3 *(continued)*

Operations Audience	Agency Audience	Print/Mail/Fullfill Audience
• Operations Manager • Mailroom Manager	• Director of Account Services • Client Services Manager • Account Supervisor	• CEO • President • Sales Manager • General Manager • Operations Manager
• Operational efficiency; • Cost savings • Security • Supply chain effectiveness • Compliance	• Customizations and creative control • Mail response rates • Speed of mail receipt • Billing accuracy • Proof of mailing	• Billing Accuracy • Proof of mailing • Competitive advantages • Relationship management

• **Proof**
  – Visibility to suppy chain compliance and performance
	• **Control**
	  – Agencies can have control over customization, delivery, reporting, rules, and billing
		• **Competitive uniqueness**
		  – Vendor allows customers to have a competitive advantage

Speed	**Speed**	**Accountability**

We are continually amazed by the failure of vendors and sellers to leverage one of their biggest hard-earned assets: their customer base. Once you have determined answers to the questions listed in the CustomerCentric Messaging Matrix, why not have people with the targeted titles within some of your loyal accounts review your messages and provide input? They will probably be flattered that their opinions are being sought, and this will help reinforce the idea that you are customer focused and remind them of the good buying decisions they made with your company; in return, you will receive input "right from the horse's mouth." This exercise can be done by territory salespeople or by tactical marketing on a national basis. If appropriate, develop unique messages for defined vertical markets or segments. Our preference in most cases is to use a rifle (vertical/title/issues) rather than a shotgun approach in trying to generate awareness and urgency. It can be useful to track which issues resonate with buyers and yield the best response rate.

To be sure, a message is a journey rather than a destination. As market conditions change, new business issues may arise, and others may become less relevant or even drop off the map. This is where the CustomerCentric Messaging Matrix may prove helpful as you refine your message based on changing market conditions and business challenges. The combination of relevant messages *and* avoiding the use of technologies in ways that emulate negative selling stereotypes should go a long way toward making your business development efforts more productive. Just as important, you facilitate the beginning of a buying experience in a way that differentiates either your salespeople or your organization. It begins by focusing on the issues that your buyers are facing and then giving them a glimpse of how they can use your offerings to help improve their business results.

Summary

The majority of customer experiences today start electronically. For executive-level buyers, offering a menu of business issues that your offerings can help them address is a way to initiate a buying cycle. By their nature, executives are not good candidates for nurturing over a long period of time.

Mid-level staff members are more likely to want to become more knowledgeable about offerings. Consider reevaluating your treatment of curious visitors. When in doubt, we suggest that you err in favor of the kinder and gentler end of the spectrum, with the goal being to facilitate a great customer experience from the start. Premature attempts to sell or qualify are inconsistent with this goal and will scare many visitors away. Of all the potential marketing usages for the Internet, we're hard pressed to think of a better one than electronic nurturing. It isn't a task that sellers can be expected to do or do well. Realize that there will be several times when you should be providing useful general information that doesn't necessarily move the buyers where you'd like them to go.

If you allow the buyer to set the pace and focus on providing a more comfortable experience while establishing a level of electronic trust over time, you have the potential to have people contact your organization when they are ready to or when they have migrated to an active need. This should also provide a steady stream of leads over time that are not tied to specific recent campaigns, but are the result of treating empowered buyers in ways that align with their levels of interest and need. There is a huge potential upside for vendors that learn to nurture curious buyers and have the patience to let them decide when their need becomes active.

STAGE 2:
RESEARCH

S ome of you may be old enough to remember Dr. Doolittle, a character in a series of children's books by Hugh Lofting. Dr. Doolittle developed an ability to speak with animals and better understand the natural world. One of the more curious animals in Dr. Doolittle's world was the pushmi-pullyu (pronounced "push-me-pull-you"), an antelope with heads at opposite ends of its body. Whenever it attempted to move, the two heads tried to go in opposite directions.

This has been what the struggle between buyers and sellers in the past decade has been like. Buyers have been fighting for control of where, how, and when they get the information that they need if they are to make informed buying decisions. On the seller's side, the historical marketing approach of placing ads, sending mail, and so on, was largely noninteractive in real time. Buyers saw or received a message, and then, if they acted, there would be a time lag before the company could respond. By that time, the urgency in the buyer's mind might have diminished, or the matter might have been expelled completely from the mind slot in favor of something more urgent. This was a "push" marketing world, where information traveled only one way: from sellers to buyers. Generally speaking, buying research took place only after the buyer's interest or curiosity had been piqued by a salesperson. Thus, the salesperson was in a position to provide as much of the information for the research as he was capable of providing. Naturally, this information was biased toward his own offering, placing him comfortably in Column A.

The Internet changed all that. Buyers could search anytime, anywhere for the information they wanted. If they couldn't find it from a particular company's Web site, alternatives were just a few clicks away. Unlike the hassles of fighting traffic across town to go to another store, there was no problem in moving from one Web site to the next until a buyer found what she was looking for. This initiated the world of "pull" buying.

All buyers conduct varying amounts of research during B2B buying cycles, with the time and effort invested being based upon the importance and complexity of the buying decision. Early on, research is used to determine options and alternatives, to find people who have common challenges, or to find those who are subject experts in areas the buyer is concerned about. This is nothing new. What is new, and remarkable, is how the Internet has empowered buyers and dramatically altered the salesperson's role in the buying cycle in such a short period of time. Buyers have eagerly embraced the new environment. For the most part, however, selling organizations have been slow to respond to these changes, often just using old tactics delivered in new ways. In today's world, alternatives are just a click away for buyers who don't perceive the seller as being helpful—as defined by the buyer!

To better understand how much the buying process has changed in such a short period of time, let's compare pre- and post-Internet research by having you join us for a trip back to the last decade.

Pre-Internet Research

It is 1993, and the start-up company you joined six years ago is doing well. Its desktop laser printers have been so well received by many companies in North America that the decision was made to establish a presence in the pan-European market. Engineering has made the necessary changes to meet the different specifications, the printers have been tested, and everything is a go from their end. Your VP of sales has begun initial discussions with potential resellers in the U.K., France, Italy, Germany, and Spain.

As VP of marketing, you are given an assignment to support the expansion that you haven't ever considered before. There is huge market share and revenue potential in Europe, but the launch will require the translation of user documentation, brochures, and technical information into French, Italian, German, and Spanish for your resellers. This is a major undertaking, and your company has no internal resources to get the job done. You leave the meeting excited about the prospects of becoming a global company, but concerned about how to go about getting all of the necessary documentation translated. You have a lot riding on making the European launch a success.

You call a friend who works for a larger company that is already doing business internationally. During the conversation, you are introduced to a new term: *language localization*. You now have the name of your assignment, if not any idea of how to accomplish it. Your friend goes on to say that his firm now has an internal translation department, but when it started doing business internationally, he believes it hired a company to perform the necessary translations. The task went beyond literal translations, as there was also the aspect of being sure that the material that buyers would see was socially correct for each country. He shared the General Motors gaffe of introducing the Chevy Nova into Spanish-speaking countries, where *no va* translates as "doesn't go." You suddenly realize that your list of translations has been expanded to five. There will have to be changes to your documentation even for material for the U.K. market.

After the call, you go to the Yellow Pages and look under "language localization." You find no listings, so you go to "translation" and find a few companies listed. You see a company name that you recognize, jot down the number, and prepare some notes for describing the engagement, the material that will need to be translated, the priority of languages, and estimated dates for the product launches in each country. You place the call and, after a brief conversation, agree to have a salesperson meet with you next week. That afternoon, your assistant brings you a fax of the salesperson's company overview. This represents all that you know about this potential vendor.

The salesperson, Susan, gives you an idea of how the process will work and explains the advantages and challenges of having in-country translations done. She also points out that her company would make every effort to find people with technical backgrounds, as their familiarity with the English text and terms would have a significant impact on the quality of the localization. When pressed, the salesperson acknowledges that not all of the translators would necessarily be employees. Often freelancers are contracted on a project-by-project basis. She offers assurances that her company uses only people who have established a track record of delivering high-quality translations and being able to adhere to schedules. She asks for copies of sample materials that will have to be localized. After reviewing them for detail and complexity, she will then be able to ballpark both the cost and the lead times that will be needed for each language. Susan ends the meeting by sharing with you that if the translations are either of poor quality or late, the investment in product launches could be adversely affected regardless of how the printers performed. You understand that a false step in introducing the products in Europe could cost your company millions of dollars and severely damage any thoughts of further global expansion.

The meeting ends with an exchange of business cards. After Susan leaves, you realize that you learned a great deal during the meeting and that it is clear that she has a good understanding of the localization business. You will have to get a detailed proposal that includes pricing, tasks to be performed, scheduling, how to go about maintaining foreign materials as changes take place in your offerings, and so on. There is also the thought that employees of the resellers that are recruited could be used to do translations, but given all that is riding on the project, your preference would be to contract with a company specializing in that space.

Over the course of the next few weeks, the salesperson from the localization company meets with you two additional times and has several phone calls to clarify some of your requirements and issues. Finally, she comes on-site to present her firm's recommendations, complete with a schedule that includes activities and time frames for their completion in each language. She introduces a project manager who helped develop the proposal and would also serve as your company's primary contact. You are impressed by the thoroughness of the proposal and feel comfortable that this salesperson understands the business and your needs and will be able to deliver on the promises made. The project manager gives his background and some of the projects for which he has been responsible and leaves no doubt of his competence and commitment if the company is chosen.

Your next meeting is with your CFO, who has to authorize the budget for the localization effort. Largely because of the thorough recommendations that the seller has made, you are able to address questions that arise. There is a lot riding on this project for your company, and you are comfortable that the vendor would do a good job. Toward the end of the meeting, however, your CFO asks a question that takes you by surprise: "Bob, you've done a good job in getting up to speed with what it's going to take, and I believe this vendor would do a good job for us. Still, it is a large expenditure. I'm curious, what other companies have you looked at?" You sheepishly answer that you have looked at only this one vendor, and you suddenly realize that you didn't come fully prepared for this meeting.

The CFO looks a little disappointed and ends the meeting by saying: "At this point, we have to get a sense of whether this pricing is reasonable and how this vendor compares to others. I think the company you've spoken with is viable and has made a detailed recommendation, but on a transaction of this size and importance, we have to make an informed decision. Get at least two other bids on this job so that we can make comparisons. You handle meetings with the other vendors. I don't want to meet with salespeople unless I absolutely have to. Get back to me once you have other quotes in the next week or so. We have to get the ball rolling on this project. We should be able to agree on which vendor we think is the best choice and negotiate the best price we can."

Your new mission and deadline are clear. You have to find at least two other vendors and get proposals from them within a week, while doing whatever you need to in order to keep them away from the CFO. You feel an understandable allegiance to Susan. Over the course of several meetings, she has brought you along in understanding what is involved in this localization project. The term *FIGS* has been added to your vocabulary of acronyms, and you find yourself no longer saying "French, Italian, German, and Spanish." Despite the extra effort required to bring in other vendors, it is the only way you can validate the recommendation, but, just as important, make certain that Susan's pricing is competitive.

You go back to your desk and try to organize your thoughts before contacting other salespeople. Susan has spent a fair amount of time educating you about the whole localization process. Your interactions with other vendors will be much shorter and to the point because you are in a hurry and you need them to provide quotes for comparisons. They won't have as much time to make a recommendation as Susan did because of your impending deadline. All things being equal, you would like to award Susan the business. You then sketch out your requirements list and see that it is nearly a mirror image of what Susan has helped you determine. You leave blank columns for the other vendors that you will be inviting to bid (see Figure 4-1).

Requirements	Column A	Column B	Column C
_____	_____		
_____	_____		
_____	_____		
_____	_____		
_____	_____		
_____	_____		
_____	_____		
_____	_____		
_____	_____		
_____	_____		
_____	_____		
_____	_____		
_____	_____		
_____	_____		
_____	_____		

Figure 4-1 *Requirements Grid*

You look through the Yellow Pages and call two other companies. These calls are dramatically different from the initial call you had with Susan. You are in a hurry. You tell them that you have budget for a localization job, and you want to make a decision in the next week or so. You ask each seller for a ballpark per word translation cost. While Susan had to ask for (and help form) them, you now give the sellers the specs, languages required, and some sample documentation, and you tell them that you need quotes ASAP.

We've just described pre-Internet research for a B2B offering. Buyers at times struggled to know even what vendors to contact if they were unfamiliar with the market or the offering. Essentially, the only ways in which vendors could create awareness with buyers were through trade shows, print ads, direct mail, or, if they were lucky, word of mouth. The ads and direct mail were valuable only as long as the prospect kept the material on her desk. Vendors had all the information, and so buyers had no choice but to contact salespeople early in the process. This was a time when the first vendor contacted enjoyed a *huge* advantage so long as the buyer concluded that that vendor was sincere and competent. By virtue of being "Column A," this vendor could establish a relationship with the buyer. Skilled salespeople could skew the requirements list toward their strengths and/or their competitors' weaknesses. It wasn't that unusual for buyers to ask the Column A salesperson to suggest other vendors to consider. The research phase ended when the requirements provided by Columns B and C had been filled out and their proposals had been submitted.

When the buyer was doing research in this way, a salesperson who could establish himself as Column A became, in effect, a buyer's research assistant. In the story we just shared, Susan was able to demonstrate that she understood her business, your business and, ultimately, your requirements. She invested time in familiarizing you with the necessary activities and the expertise required to execute them. The proposal she provided addressed and defined your requirements and became the yardstick against which other proposals would be measured. Vendors B and C, while delighted to be invited to bid, faced an uphill battle. You would not have the patience to start from ground zero with them as you did with Susan. They didn't have the same opportunity to establish their sincerity and competence. You really just wanted them to provide a quote because you were now more of an "expert buyer." You also had an understandable bias toward doing business with Susan's company.

There is usually good news and bad news for Vendors B and C. The good news is that this will be a short sales cycle (Susan has done virtually all the selling). The bad news is that the other vendors will put in the effort to expedite the proposal despite not having all the information they need, only to learn that they didn't get the business.

Today's Research Process

Consider how doing research on offerings has changed. Can you even find a copy of the Yellow Pages in your office? Do you have a Rolodex on your desk with all of your contacts? Probably not, you say, but you do have your contacts in Outlook or some other device. Are these the contacts you turn to when you have to research a need? More than likely, you turn to the Internet, where it doesn't matter whom you do or don't know. You can remedy that problem in minutes by finding your "tribe" of other like-minded people. If you have a free account on LinkedIn, for example, a simple key-word search can identify people who have experience in whatever you may be interested in. From there, getting introduced is an easy matter, and you now have a virtual relationship, without ever having had to attend a trade show to pick up the business card. Of course, you didn't get to earn those frequent flyer miles either.

Perhaps your Internet search led you to a blog post that had earned several comments. You know nothing about the blog author, or blogger, but as you scan the comments, you see that there are many other people who care about the same issue and have opinions and experiences that you don't. This helps to form your opinions, which, subconsciously, are forming your buying criteria. You post a comment or a question, and you now belong. You click on the RSS feed so that you are kept in the loop by receiving all responses or comments. You're now part of the dialogue, and you'll have gone from knowing nothing to knowing a fair amount by the time you first speak with a vendor. And all the while, the vendor's salesperson has had no contact with you and, as a result, may play a less valuable role in your decision-making process. During this research phase, the buyer often sees the salesperson as unnecessary. Given their preconceptions about salespeople, buyers attempt to gather as much information as possible so that they can just place the order and avoid what they perceive as the typical "sales dance."

Having a buyer just call and place an order may sound like good news to many salespeople. But it's not good news to the multiple vendors who don't get the call. As we progress through this chapter, we will discuss what you can do to better position yourself not only to get the call, but to guide the buyer through the increasingly virtual buying process.

The Internet has empowered buyers to perform research much more efficiently and thoroughly, but it's not perfect. If anything, the problem has become information overload. The challenge has become paring down the information to determine your needs and choose which vendors will be invited to bid. Just as important, the problem becomes whom to trust. True, you may have found a lot of information and a lot of opinions, but can those opinions be trusted? What do you really know about those people and their experiences? What is it that makes us trust and believe what we read online . . . as long as it wasn't written by a salesperson? Or was it? Who's to say that the salesperson cannot be the expert blogger, or the person who has the most credible comment on the blog? He can be, and, as you'll learn, this gives many sellers the opportunity to give the buyers exactly what they are looking for.

The business situations that arise today are not much different from those that arose 10 or 20 years ago, but the ease and thoroughness of researching ways to address them has progressed at lightning speed. Technology has enabled instant access to and sharing of information, and this has empowered buyers like never before. This empowerment has come at a price to sellers and vendors, who now have a greatly reduced ability to influence requirements and buying decisions. The primary reason is that buyers can now progress much farther into buying cycles before interacting with salespeople.

Let's revisit the need to find a language localization vendor, but roll the calendar ahead to today's buyers. After learning about the requirement to translate all materials into four different languages, the first step would be to use a search engine to learn what vendors there are in this space that warrant your consideration. After the meeting, you arrive at your office and do a Google search by typing "English translations for companies doing business in Europe." Then, 0.24 second later, you have "about 230,000" returns. You click on the first one, which we'll call Acme Language Translation (of course!).

The Acme Web site provides a list of services, and you quickly see that language localization is the task at hand and that this company lists 10 vertical markets that it serves, with Information Technology being one of them. By clicking on that vertical, you learn that it lists Techtronix, a printer manufacturer, as one of its clients. There is a link to a case study, which you click on and peruse.

You backspace a few pages to the Google search return and click on the next site, yet another company in the space, and you begin to see very similar information. One difference is that this Web site has an electronic form that you can submit to get a price estimate. You start to complete the form, but you decide that you aren't ready to provide your contact information just yet. You fear that if you do, a salesperson will call.

You wind up accessing five Web sites, meaning that you have identified five companies that could bid on your job. Each of the Web sites has similar content, and you find a diminishing value in each new one you have seen.

Since this is an important project, you open Yahoo!, thinking that you'll get different results, and type in "Acme Language Translation" to see anything that's been written about the company. The first few returns are connected to the main Acme Web site, but one return catches your eye. You click on it and go to a YouTube video that features Acme. The video showcases Acme's services, is professional, and gives you a good feeling about the company's abilities.

Rather than continue to visit other sites, you do another search by typing: "language localization vendors." In 0.23 second, you get 88,400 returns. You look at the first few links, and a Web site offering free localization insight is listed. It doesn't appear to be linked to any vendors, and you spend about 10 minutes perusing several topics. It offers PDF documents showing the five major reasons that localization projects fail, the benefits of single-sourcing jobs, and a link to technical translation jobs that you download so that you can read it later. You then see 10 topics covered in blogs and review the ones that are of most interest.

After considering your research experience, which was spread over two or three days, you've developed a list of your requirements:

- A single vendor to handle all languages.

- The ability to review résumés of all translators that would do the work.

- An understanding of the TMS (Translation Management System) that will be used.

- Vendors must have experience translating Web sites.

- Vendors must be financially secure.

- You want the ability to interview the project manager that a vendor would assign to your account.

- Ongoing support of translations.

- Vendor references from technology companies for which they have done projects.

Based upon these requirements, you will choose the vendors that provide the best match to your criteria. The key difference compared to pre-Internet research is that no salesperson has been contacted, and, therefore, *no salesperson has influenced your buying criteria.* This means that there is no "Column A" that has shaped your requirements and established himself as the person you would prefer to do business with (allow to win a tie). You can also see that during the research phase, if you are a vendor that the buyer hadn't considered before, her buying experience began electronically with a Web site visit. Just as salespeople make an impression, visitors draw certain conclusions about your company and offerings from the "look and feel" of your Web site and, much more important, how instrumental the Web site was in helping the buyer. In the research phase, a buyer is vulnerable, and being helpful builds loyalty.

In your search for vendors, not one of them has distinguished itself through the Web site experience, as they all seemed about the same. The language localization Web site provided what you felt was the most valuable (and hopefully unbiased) information. It has been your major source for establishing your requirements list.

Buyers who are active in social networking have the option of polling their network of trusted people at any time during a buying cycle. Buyers utilizing the Internet for research are fully aware that vendors buy search engine positions and that all information on Web sites is "pushed" to them by vendors that control the content. Any hyperbole, including customer testimonials, will be taken with a grain of salt. You would hope that all vendors have some satisfied customers. Buyers would prefer to know what average or unhappy customers have to say about vendors and their offerings, but they know that those quotes will never appear on a vendor Web site. So how can they find them? Quite easily, as it turns out.

In Chapter 2, we mentioned that it is often said that an unhappy customer will tell 13 people. In the past, vendors could easily hide unhappy customers from prospective buyers unless the buyer happened to know someone who had had a direct experience with the vendor. Today, if that unhappy customer is a blogger with a sizable following, his Web site is likely to have a high page rank because of the many external sites linking to his, making the site easier to find. A readership in the thousands is not unlikely. Hypothetically, let's say that the blogger has had an unpleasant experience with Acme Language Translation. He writes a post—not scathing, but generally negative. He titles the post (using an H1 tag to increase search optimization) Acme Language Translation Review. Naturally, if you type that phrase into the most popular search engines, his blog entry will come up first. And that's what an astute buyer will see.

Just as commonly, it doesn't even have to be a blog post. Many Internet users belong to message groups and receive e-mails from the group as new postings are made. In this communication stream, it is very easy for anyone to make a comment about a company that is unfiltered and distributed to the thousands or hundreds of thousands of subscribers. And, unlike spam from vendors, these e-mails get opened and read.

As stated previously, everyone is a publisher with the Internet. *This can work for or against market leaders.* Take CRM, for example, where Salesforce.com has established itself as a market leader with substantial market penetration. However, a quick Web search could lead you to a blog such as www.gripeforce.blogspot.com, which is dedicated to any and all problems with the CRM application. And so the buyer has to sift through the mountain of data to make an informed decision.

Social networking can be used throughout the research phase. In the initial stages, you could seek recommended vendors or general advice or guidance related to language localization. Later in the research effort, you could leverage your network by broadcasting a description of your situation and requirements to allow people to comment not only on what you are looking for, but also on what companies they can recommend or suggest that you avoid. If a particular company receives a glowing recommendation, you'll have to consider whether the recommendation is genuine or from a "plant"—

someone who is aligned with the company being recommended. Likewise, if a company is criticized, you'll have to contemplate whether this negative review was offered by a competing salesperson. The Internet makes getting information easier, but it doesn't necessarily make it easier to make decisions.

Toward the end of the research phase, you could solicit opinions on the vendors that you are considering for your short list and provide an opportunity for any eleventh-hour additions (or deletions). Opinions and input received via social networking are highly valued as long as you know or trust the source. People you have relationships with that have no financial stake in which vendor you choose are providing transparent information.

As you can see in Figure 4-2, the requirements column does not represent the offerings of any single vendor; rather, it is a composite of all the research that you've performed, including Web site visits, blogs, social networking, and so on. For that reason, there is no "Column A" salesperson or vendor that has shaped the requirements and reaped a huge competitive advantage by doing so. Vendors 1, 2, and 3 (or more) just represent the companies the buyer has decided to consider. This will mean contacting the salespeople, and probably requesting proposals or bids from them. Relating to the buying curves model, this means that when the buyer talks with these salespeople, she will already be in Phase 2 because the requirements are known.

We don't want to infer that a salesperson's job is now to wait for the phone to ring and blindly provide quotes for whatever buyers believe their requirements are. This research is a result of buyers being tired of vendors taking advantage of them by hyping or lying about their offerings. For a complex offering, the buyer's requirements are unlikely to be complete or accurate. By that we mean that there will be missing requirements, things that the buyer had not considered. There may be requirements that don't belong. The initial encounter a seller has with a self-educated and empowered buyer, however, is dramatically different, and traditional selling behavior will be out of alignment with the buyer.

REQUIREMENTS	VENDOR 1	VENDOR 2	VENDOR 3

Figure 4-2

Aligning Selling Approaches with the Buyer's Research Behavior

As in the example of choosing a language localization provider, there is a great deal of research that has to be done in investigating B2B offerings of any complexity. But who is doing the research, and what is her role in the buying process? While there were only two people involved in the example provided, B2B opportunities typically have several committee members, each with his own preconceived notions, personal agendas, and perspectives. A major factor in the difficulty of selling is determined by how many areas of the business an offering touches. The extreme would be an enterprise resource planning (ERP) system that touches accounting, manufacturing, purchasing, engineering, and other areas. As a comparison, if a company were considering outsourcing its payroll, the committee would represent far fewer stakeholders.

Let's look at four different B2B buyers and understand that buying cycles, or at least curiosity, can begin at any level:

- Business buyers will be interested in learning about business issues that can be addressed, other companies in their space that have bought the offering, results that have been achieved, the vendor's financial stability and position in the marketplace, and its reputation for service and support. *Information that is too granular will overwhelm them.*

- Midlevel managers will be more concerned about *implementation*: how a new approach may affect their people, what impact it will have on their budget, expectations that will be set for results, and how it will affect their specific areas of responsibility.

- Infrastructure staff members who will have to implement a new offering (e.g., IT staff with regard to new application software) will generally not have perspective on areas of the business that can be positively affected. Their view is more personal in trying to determine whether an offering will *make their jobs easier* and whether *end users will be happy with it*. There is also consideration for core competencies and the potential impact on staff within their own departments.

- End users are almost entirely focused on whether or not a new offering will *make their jobs easier* and whether they could face any *loss of stature* in their organization as a result of implementing a new offering. They are concerned about reliability, support, training, and other such areas. They also prefer doing business with established market leaders rather than niche players, as potential future employment opportunities will be greater for offerings that are widely used.

As you can see, the task of attracting and developing potential buyers in the three different categories (latent need, curious, and active need) can and should be different based upon the level the person has reached within his organization.

To add to the complexity of research, there are factors other than the offering and the price that must be considered and can strongly influence buying decisions:

- A strong reputation for support in implementations can allow vendors to overcome deficiencies in their offerings and win. Having additional bells and whistles in offerings is not helpful if they never get implemented and used.

- Professional support for areas where you lack certain core competencies that are necessary during a project. Many late market buyers want a single point of contact in acquiring these services directly from the vendor providing the offering.

- Vendors' perceived position in the marketplace and financial stability. Buyers want this information before they make significant commitments. If applications or capabilities are mission-critical for buyers, they will look to vendors that can demonstrate a track record and stability.

- A vendor's reputation for maintenance, repair, and upgrade policies, if applicable.

- A vendor's reputation for how it treats customers. Has it shown a pattern of aggressively withdrawing support from older offerings to steer customers toward buying new announcements?

- For committee decisions, each buyer may have a personal agenda related to how a particular vendor could affect her position, power, and career.

Seldom does a vendor dominate in all these categories, so it is important for a vendor to be perceived as strong in the categories that are most important to the highest-level buyers. What becomes clear is that visitors coming to your Web site have different descriptions and agendas:

- A person with an active need that your company created through an ad or campaign

- A curious buyer that came because of an ad or campaign from your company

- A buyer who is already committed to evaluate offerings in your space who found you via a Web search

- A buyer who has spoken with a seller and is looking for other columns

- A lower-level buyer who has been told to look

When it comes to content on Web sites, one size does not fit all. General information will yield disappointing results for most visitors.

The Sales Plan: Positioning Yourself to Win the Research Phase

Companies spend huge sums of money on their offerings to establish or maintain competitive advantages. Yet, if they fail to distinguish themselves during the research phase, they may never make buyers' short lists. During the research phase, buyers want anonymous and credible information (both general and specific to your offerings), without the usual vendor hype.

They want the ability to determine the pace and the level of detail of their evaluations without being "qualified" by your Web site, and they want to decide if and when they are ready to be contacted by a salesperson. Despite the differences that we discussed in the stereotypical traits of people involved in sales and marketing, sales habits have seeped into most Web sites, probably because the desired outcomes are leads. Corporate cultures lean toward driving top-line revenues by selling, not by empowering buyers to buy. Organizations that fail to change will drift further and further out of alignment with the new breed of buyers.

As soon as buyers feel that they are "being sold," defensive behavior takes over. Have you ever found yourself browsing in a retail store mulling over whether or not to buy a particular item and been asked by a clerk: "May I help you?" How often does that question cause you to move along, ending any possibility of buying that item? So it is with Web sites as well.

We are aware that some companies allow the initial contact with a curious buyer to be someone other than a salesperson. It may be a support or application expert who can better address implementation issues or technical questions. More important, such a person isn't a commissioned seller that will be trying quickly and overtly to qualify the prospect.

In the same way that superior salespeople differentiate themselves by how they sell (or allow people to buy), company Web sites can do the same. A few questions to consider:

- Is your Web site about your company or about how your clients are using your offerings?

- Do you have a way of assessing the level (executive, middle management, infrastructure, or user) of visitors and aligning with them by providing the type of information they'd like to see?

- Do you offer information (electronic newsletter, Webinars, white papers, or other such data) that provides value to visitors and fosters a "sticky" electronic relationship? Are you *sure* that the visitors value the information? How do you know?

- What conclusions would you like Web site visitors to make about your company, and how are you trying to earn those opinions?

- If someone were to visit your Web site and those of your two major competitors, which buyer experience would stand out? Which company will buyers perceive as most helpful?

Many of these questions relate to the buyer's experience with your company Web site but, as we described earlier, a buyer will be exposed to many areas of influence other than your Web site during his research phase. How well are you positioned in those areas? Here are a few more questions for you to ponder:

- How many members of your team (sales, marketing, and executives) are respected bloggers that publish helpful (rather than biased) information?

- Do you have a staff member who is responsible for daily or continually performing complex Web searches to find out what is being said about you and your competitors?

- If you are a salesperson, do you belong to every newsgroup that your buyers are likely to subscribe to so that you can read what is being said? If so, have you positioned yourself as a trusted advisor of information with frequent posts? Do you include your contact information in each post so that a buyer in the research phase can contact you when she finds your posts?

- Has your company attempted to create "independent" Web communities (portals) to facilitate an exchange of information about a particular topic (language translation, for example)? Does this portal retain its independence and allow discussion about competitors and alternatives? As the portal "sponsor," have you succeeded in positioning your company as helpful, trustworthy, and the definitive source for information on the topic?

- Do you have basic Google alerts set up to inform you of any news related to areas that you should be interested in (your company, your competitors, key phrases, and so on)?

- Do you survey buyers in your pipeline to find out what they search on in the research phase? Do you use this information to (a) optimize key pages on your Web site, (b) buy search placement ads based on these key phrases, and (c) analyze what high-ranking results appear as a result of these search phrases and compare them with your messaging?

This is not meant to be a complete list of questions. Rather, it is meant to get you, and your team, thinking.

Summary

The buying process has changed. Nowhere is this more apparent than in the research phase. Yet, vendors are not helpless. In fact, we believe the changes brought on by technology present an unprecedented opportunity for sellers to take positive action. While it's easy for buyers to find a mountain of information, it's equally easy for sellers to understand what buyers are looking for and to provide that information in an unbiased, helpful manner. It takes an investment in time and a focus on execution to do so.

If we had to name a single attribute of a superior as compared to an average seller, it would be this: patience. Superior sellers have the patience to ask questions, not discuss offerings too soon, avoid premature price discussions, not close before buyers are ready, and so on. For visitors who are coming to your Web site during the research/nurturing stage, having them feel that your site was patient and helpful would set you apart from most of your competitors, and would make those visitors want to keep coming back. And that's what you want.

STAGE 3:
PREFERENCES

pref·er·ence [pref-er-uhns, pref-ruhns] (1) that which is preferred; choice; (2) the power or opportunity of choosing one that is preferred

If a buyer begins a buying cycle with no knowledge of vendors' products or reputations, then how are buying preferences determined? How has technology supported changes in the way in which preferences are formed? What role does the salesperson play in establishing buyer preferences?

For the moment, let's assume that the buyer starts a buying cycle with no familiarity with potential vendors, as was the case with the language translation example in Chapter 4. This is an important distinction because of the impact that conscious and subconscious brand awareness has on buyer preferences. Branding is a critically important strategic objective for businesses, but it is beyond the scope of this book. For this reason, we'll assume brand equality and that the buyer has no preconceived preferences.

We believe that business buyers are interested in making buying decisions that allow them to visualize doing one of the following:

1. Achieving a goal

2. Solving a problem

3. Satisfying a need

Buyers may not articulate these criteria, but you can be assured that their motivation for buying will fall into one of these categories. You probably have your own buying experiences that you can compare to these categories. Whether it is an expensive car that needs to be rationalized or a goal imposed by the CEO to achieve a certain level of revenue growth, buyers' decisions are ultimately based on which offering best *allows* them to visualize achieving a goal, solving a problem, or satisfying a need.

People Buy from People

An interesting perception of business-to-business (B2B) buying is that companies are buying from companies. While this is technically true, it isn't really the case. The buying organization is made up of people. Before they arrive at work and after they go home, buyers are people, with emotions and experiences that drive how they think, act, feel, and respond, and at what pace. The same applies to the people who make up selling organizations. People don't get to work and then become other people, such as "professional buyers." It is true that their job may be to buy and spend money, but the way they form preferences and opinions within companies is largely the same as the way they do it on the outside. Things that make them happy in their private lives (humor, esprit de corps, and isolation, for example) also make them happy at work. Similarly, things that upset them in their private lives (disorganization or lack of perceived respect, for example) also cause them grief in a professional setting.

One of the primary differences between B2B and B2C buying relates to the dynamics of buying committees, which are, of course, largely absent or less formal in personal buying decisions. However, when you look closely, isn't most of the buyer behavior on committees largely driven by the emotional profiles of each constituent? Some want to impress and stand alone. These are the buyers who exert great influence and may take more risk. If you are in sales, they can be your champions, or they can be your worst enemies. Other committee members may be more inclined to want to be perceived as being cooperative and interested in consensus. They have the same attributes in their private lives. They are safe and more cautious. They too can be your champion or your roadblock, depending on what the buyer is trying to achieve.

The point is that, ultimately, people buy from people. Buying preferences may have a rational, logical, programmatic component, but they definitely have an emotional component as well. This means that it is critical to understand the buyer's unique situation as early as possible in the sales process and not necessarily treat all buyers the same way. It is true that there are a lot of general commonalities that buyers of a particular offering will have, and that those commonalities can be used in early demand generation messaging to create interest and awareness. But as the buyer approaches the point of contact, the selling organization has to become less of a hospital (come here if you hurt) and more of a doctor (let me listen to you, so that I can diagnose).

Case Study: Forming Buying Preferences

As an example of how buying preferences are formed, consider the following story in which you are the main character. By the way, congratulations! You've been promoted to VP of sales!

You've spent countless hours with your sales operations manager researching the CRM systems that are available in the market. This has included Web searches, visits to different Web sites, trade show visits, blogs, listening to live and recorded Webinars, and leveraging people you trust within your social network. You have defined what you believe are your requirements, and you have created a list of five vendors that you plan to contact. You've been careful to include the "gorilla in the space" as well as one relatively new vendor.

Up to this point, it has been both unnecessary and undesirable for you to have direct contact with any salespeople, but you realize that this has to change. You now want to be able to analyze the strengths and weaknesses of vendors and their offerings, services, support, and implementation help, and, ultimately, to get quotes from vendors that you feel can address your requirements. You plan to have three or four vendors on your short list, meaning that you will eliminate one or two. This decision was due in part to your feeling that reviewing as many as five proposals would be overwhelming.

Unlike in buying decisions made several years ago, you are not looking for (nor will you tolerate) attempts by any of these sellers to educate you on their offerings. Nor will you tolerate "old school" stereotypical sales approaches. You have spent a fair amount of time familiarizing yourself with what is available. Any salesperson who attempts to start from the beginning will be wasting your time and will not align with your objectives for the call. Your hope is that any seller you talk with will quickly determine that you've done your homework and react accordingly. Attempts to force any features into your requirements list will meet with strong resistance and objections. You would like your questions addressed with a minimal amount of hype, and you want to exert a reasonable amount of control over the discussion during the sales calls.

The decision will be fairly complex. For starters, there are four people on the buying committee: the VP of marketing, the CFO, the CIO, and yourself (the VP of sales). You will place high value on the opinions of your sales operations manager, who will have far more direct contact with the offering than you will. The committee members will have varying degrees of involvement with the new CRM system, may have differing opinions about which vendor to choose, and will have their own agendas for what will be accomplished by using the new system. Beyond evaluating each offering, there will be several areas to consider for each vendor:

- The support offered for implementing the new system

- IT support in migrating from your legacy sales force automation (SFA) system

- Financial stability

- Experience in your market segment

- References that can be checked

- The ability to customize the system to fit your environment (including pipeline milestones)

- User acceptance, education, and support

- The buying experience with the seller and the company

- Terms and conditions

- Cost versus functionality

As VP of sales, you feel that your opinion should carry the day, but you know that your CFO will be concerned about cost and forecasting accuracy. Likewise, the VP of marketing will be most interested in the ability to manage and track campaigns, while the CIO will want minimal disruption in making the transition to the new system. The vendors you've chosen have hosted offerings, so after the initial conversion, IT efforts and support will be minimal. You are confident that the CIO will not want to attempt to develop her own software. Even individual sales managers and salespeople will have preferences based upon opinions or experience with different vendors. It may be helpful to get support from some opinion leaders for the vendor you would like to do business with.

Your sales operations manager will be involved in all the initial meetings, including some that you may not be able to attend. Your CFO doesn't have time to meet with any salespeople, and you would like to decide which ones should meet with the VP of marketing.

Live Sales Contact

The first salesperson meets with your sales operations manager and you. He seems to be trying a bit too hard to get both of you to like him and spending more time on establishing rapport than you felt was appropriate. His company introduction was fairly rote, and he quickly offered many opinions as to why his offering was user-friendly, even though you hadn't indicated that this was one of your concerns. Notable by its absence was curiosity about why you were considering CRM and what your requirements were based upon the research that you had done.

He quickly signed online and began to walk you through the different screens to show how sellers would input information to keep the pipeline current. You saw how anyone within an organization could quickly get up to speed concerning interactions with a given client by any members of the sales or support team. He also demonstrated how marketing could pass leads to salespeople, track them, and analyze the results of a campaign.

The management reports showed how the activity in and strength of the pipeline could be assessed at the rep, manager, regional, and company levels. Forecasting could be done by applying each rep's historical close rates to defined milestones and projecting revenue figures. Strangely enough, your sales operations manager had already seen many of the screens during visits to the company Web site.

The salesperson began to close the meeting by asking how many people you wanted to support, what type of effort would be involved in defining milestones to fit your transactions, and whether you would want professional services support to migrate legacy data to populate the new CRM system. He said that he would provide a detailed price quotation within a few days and asked how his offering compared to others you had seen. It was a fairly naked qualification question that your sales operations manager could answer honestly and tersely: "You are the first salesperson we've met with." He spent the next few minutes giving you the "why you should do business with us" speech and then wrapped up the call.

This initial call was replicated three more times. You and your sales operations manager felt that all of the calls were more about the vendors' offerings and less about what your requirements were. Despite the amount of research you had done collectively, all the sellers treated you as novice buyers. The demos all caused the sellers to act like windup dolls, as it was clear that they had done them hundreds of times. After the calls, it was hard to distinguish one offering from another. All the screens, brochures, Web sites, and sellers tended to run together. It was difficult to say that any of the sellers added value or insights to your evaluation of CRM.

How Salespeople Can Win Preferential Status

Linda was different almost from the handshake. She dressed and acted in a professional manner and seemed more intent on displaying competence than in getting us to like her (which we did). It was refreshing that she aligned more closely in discovering our objectives for the call in that she

- Asked us if we knew about her company or wanted a brief overview.

- Had done her homework by knowing what type of offerings we sold and sharing some results that a client in a similar space to ours had achieved.

- Did not bring a laptop to the initial sales call.

- Asked detailed questions about our current system, our sales cycles, the milestones we used, and levels of acceptance by the sales force, as well as their likes and dislikes.

- Gave us an opportunity to share what we had determined were the requirements for a CRM system. In doing so, she respected the research that we had already done and avoided treating us like novice buyers, as the other sellers had.

- Helped uncover potential results that could be positively affected and quantified the potential payback that could be part of a cost versus benefit analysis.

- Raised some implementation and customization issues that neither of us had considered.

- Ended the call by saying that she would document what she believed our requirements were, and if both of us agreed, would customize a demo showing just the parts of her offering that were of interest.

When Linda left, you realized that she had raised the bar. By comparison, the other sellers had taken a "quote and hope" approach. She understood and in fact helped to clarify your requirements, while avoiding the trap of doing a demo during the first call, virtually guaranteeing a second call with the ability to offer a demo that was tailored to address your needs. She offered to facilitate a cost versus benefit analysis that would make it easier for the CFO to approve the expenditure and for you to set expectations.

Without a doubt, Linda has provided a superior buying experience to this point. Based primarily on her competence and professionalism, your sales operations manager and you have developed a preference for doing business with her. On the second call, she brings a support person who would assist in migrating legacy data and in helping to customize milestones. She and the support person do a customized demo showing the capabilities that were agreed to during the first sales call. They both provide potential areas of benefit that other clients have realized and help you quantify the value that can be realized through implementing their CRM software.

After a few additional phone calls, the proposal is provided, with a concise executive summary, a detailed implementation schedule, pricing, and a cost versus benefit analysis. At this point, you request references from all vendors that have submitted proposals.

Your sales operations manager prepares a detailed comparison of vendors and offerings, but it becomes clear that he would like to have Linda win the business. In effect, this member of your team has become a champion for Linda. As a result, the list of requirements is dominated by features from her offering. In areas where it is lacking, weighting factors can be used creatively to skew the final result. In any subjective areas, generous marks are given to justify your preference. Showing the analysis to the CFO and the VP of marketing will make Linda's company a clear choice.

Your CFO made it clear that he had no desire to meet with any of the salespeople. Prior to a committee meeting, you'd like to get your VP of marketing on board, so you arrange a meeting with Linda. You prep her for what you believe are the VP of marketing's requirements, and it comes as no surprise that the call goes well and that your recommendation will receive backing from three (those that met Linda) of the four members of the committee. Linda's price is not the lowest bid, but it is in the ballpark. Rather than broach the subject now, you'll wait until the decision is conditionally finalized before leveraging the other quotes.

Changes in Determining Preferences

Imagine for a moment how the decision on CRM would have been made if Linda had not been involved. While price and product are often cited on loss reports, the cruel reality is that the best salesperson usually wins. Without a competent salesperson's involvement, *decisions can degrade to pricing alone.*

The Internet significantly affects which vendors will ultimately be invited to compete for a given transaction. Many pre-Internet opportunities were initiated by direct selling efforts. The seller who got in first enjoyed significant advantages in that he

- Encountered a buyer who had few, if any, preconceived notions about requirements.

- Could develop buyer requirements they were biased toward his company's strengths and the weaknesses of potential competitors that could be brought in later, in much the same way that RFPs get "wired" by the vendor that initiates them.

- Could usually keep competition out of the opportunity until the buying cycle was far enough along so that other salespeople had a minimal chance to change the requirements.

- Was often asked what vendors should be considered so that comparisons could be made.

- Would be given an opportunity to respond to lower quotes. It was and is common in situations where there is a Column A salesperson for buyers to give that salesperson a last look in order to either match the price or come close to where it would have to be to win the transaction.

In this situation, it was far easier for industry leaders to continue dominating, in large part because it was difficult for buyers to find alternatives.

To fully appreciate how selling and buying have changed and how frequently there is no Column A, imagine receiving a compelling voice mail from a salesperson you don't know about an offering that addresses a high-priority business issue that you didn't know how to address. Despite having your interest piqued by that enterprising salesperson, would you

- Return the call?

- Do an online search?

An increasing percentage of buyers would choose the second option. Even if you visit the Web site of the seller who initiates the buying cycle, it is possible that she won't make your short list if the electronic buying experience at her firm's site isn't up to par with that on other sites you access. We are aware of some vendors that post detailed information and even pricing on their Web sites. They have helped to justify a buyer's decision by serving as a "column" without ever having a salesperson talk or meet with the client.

According to the Sales Benchmark Index research on world-class sales organizations, on average, WCSOs have 57 percent fewer leads entering their pipelines that are generated by territory salespeople. SBI offers two reasons for this statistic:

- Centralized business development efforts fueled by formal campaigns and cost-justified by past results are *more effective* than ad hoc efforts by individual salespeople.

- Territory salespeople have more time to focus on moving opportunities along in the pipeline when they are relieved of some of the business development burden.

We'd like to add a few opinions as to why this statistic applies to WCSOs:

- Prospecting appears to be very low on the list of skills that salespeople are able and willing to apply across virtually all organizations.

- Given annual quota pressure, salespeople are unable to nurture many prospects.

- Senior executives want their salespeople focused on closing short-term deals, not on nurturing long-term prospects.

- The cost of sales for nurturing can be prohibitive unless it is done electronically.

- Over time, buyers' electronic buying experiences will determine which vendors will be invited to bid when an organization is ready to consider buying.

Senior executives, especially those of publicly traded companies, spend a great deal of time focusing on the opportunities in their sales pipelines because they are an indication of how the next month or quarter is going to look from a revenue recognition standpoint. Providing visibility and guidance to investors and analysts who abhor surprises is critical in establishing credibility and maintaining share price. Our belief is that keeping and scoring curious buyers in varying stages can further improve an organization's visibility. By collecting data over time, it would be fairly straightforward to project the relative number of curious visitors that would potentially become leads over a given period of time.

How Salespeople Can Ruin Opportunities

If and when a seller is contacted by a knowledgeable buyer, alignment is a critical skill that superior sellers have intuitively. Those who are less gifted struggle because their concept and whatever formal training they have are focused on selling, not on empowering someone to buy. Assume that you had decided to buy an Audi A6 and were planning to visit three dealerships to get the best price. You drive 50 miles to the furthest dealer (you hope the one closest to you will be able to match or beat whatever price you get from the others).

The salesperson at the first dealership greets you. He then takes you over to an A6 on the lot. He opens the hood and feels compelled to let you know that the car has an overhead cam (he's mistaken you for someone who cares). He touts the 18-inch wheels (since you live in a city, you start to imagine how they'll fare with the potholes). Next he shows you the pass-through for your skis (if only you were a skier!). After the test drive, he shows you plaques for outstanding service (don't all dealers either win them or have them made?). Finally, after you have endured the sales pitch, you get to the primary objective of the visit, which is a test drive that makes a favorable impression on you. Your mission is now to get an idea of price and escape, which is difficult because the seller knows that if you leave the showroom without buying, his chances dwindle (which is actually true). However, you succeed. Without getting his pencil sharpened, you now have an idea of what you can buy the car for.

Imagine now going into the second dealership. You know the car and the features you want. It would be painful to hear a seller espouse the overhead cam, 18-inch wheels, ski pass-through, and legendary service department again. You also don't want or need to drive another A6. You really just want a price so that you can make a decision. You don't want to be subjected to any selling. You know what you want, and you take control, leaving the seller little more to do than quote a price and take his chances. The buyer's revolution has given you the upper hand.

The Sales Plan: Positioning Yourself to Win the Preference Phase

Selling was something that buyers tolerated much more in pre-Internet times because they had no alternative. Some sellers were better than others, but it was clear that the seller had an agenda as to how to influence your requirements. Today, using these sales approaches with knowledgeable buyers is the equivalent of putting obnoxiousness on performance-enhancing drugs. It will be more like an arm-wrestling contest than it is like the buying experience that people crave and are starting to demand. This is and will continue to be a challenge until more organizations and salespeople embrace the concept of empowering buyers. Sellers that don't relate to buyers quickly run the risk of not being invited to bid or merely being leveraged to get the best possible price from a seller who does relate to them.

At a minimum, sellers should consider a step that we call interest qualification when they first encounter a buyer (especially when it is a reactive contact). In the case of the second, the third, or even the first Audi salesperson, most buyers would appreciate questions about how familiar they were with the A6 before launching into the information on the overhead cam, 18-inch wheels, ski pass-through, and other such data.

In a B2B situation, this involves validating any research that a buyer has done by asking early in an initial call what the buyer has established as requirements for whatever offering he is interested in. Once those requirements have been uncovered, a logical next step would be to get a sense for what value the buyer perceives he would get from the offering being considered. Our belief is that if a buyer doesn't readily know, the seller can offer a list of business goals that can be achieved through the use of her offering. A seller gains credibility by doing so, especially if it helps the buyer realize that there are additional areas of potential savings or value that he had not considered.

Once a business issue that the buyer would like to affect has been identified, the seller has earned the right to ask the buyer a more detailed question. It would be reasonable to now ask what requirements or features the buyer believes would enable him to accomplish his stated goal. A seller will gain tremendous credibility if he is then able to ask some intelligent questions to add capabilities to the requirements list. At the extreme, he may also be able to have the buyer conclude that some of his requirements do not belong on the list.

Summary

Interest qualification facilitates better alignment by recognizing that today's buyers are likely to already be in Phase 2 of the buying cycle. Giving them a chance to express their preferences to date rather than going directly into selling mode affords buyers some control over where the call is headed and minimizes the chances that they will feel that their time is being wasted or that the seller is trying to manipulate them. If buyers are unaware of their requirements, the seller can begin to develop their needs by treating the buyer more as a novice than as an expert.

Buyers who have done research, developed requirements, and determined preferences are a reality. Vendors that embrace and align with this change stand to reap the windfall of capturing the lion's share of revenue from competitors that cling to old habits. Nurturing curious buyers electronically is a challenge. If you are successful at doing so, it would be a shame to have a buyer contact one of your sellers, only to be subjected to sales techniques focused on developing the requirements for a nonexpert buyer. It is a road to a negative buying experience and the potential of not even making the short list of vendors being considered.

6

STAGE 4: REASSURANCE

You have completed your evaluation of cars, and you feel that a Ford Fusion is the best alternative. A key criterion for you is fuel economy, and the Fusion is touted as getting 30 miles per gallon with regular gas, which is twice what your SUV delivers using premium. You've done the math based upon the 22,000 miles a year that you drive. A large part of your justification for buying the car is that you'll have no repairs for at least a couple of years, and your fuel costs will be cut in half.

The problem with these calculations is that the finances make sense only if the new car actually delivers 30 mpg for the type of driving that you do. The EPA sticker is not something that you want to rely on. You could ask the salesperson, but he wants you to buy the car and will probably say whatever he has to. You could ask for customers you can contact, but you wouldn't know what type of driving they do. You finally decide to rent a Fusion at a low weekend rate and see for yourself what mileage you can reasonably expect. When you get 32 mpg with the car, you are confident in your decision.

In making a buying decision, cost versus benefit calculations provide an understanding of the potential payback, but they are based upon assumptions. Proof is verifying that whatever you are buying will perform as advertised in your environment, or at least will meet your expectations.

Once a buyer has established a preference for a vendor or a solution, she will seek both logical and emotional reassurance that she is making the right choice—that she's leaning in the right direction. We say that she is seeking emotional reassurance because much of the observed behavior at this stage of the buying process is not based on rational logic concerning whether the decision is right or wrong. Rather, it is based on supporting a preference, or decision, that has already been tentatively made.

In 2006, Michael Lovaglia, professor and chairman of the sociology department at the University of Iowa, received recognition among bloggers for putting forth what was called Lovaglia's Law, in which he proposed:

Lovaglia's Law: The more important the outcome of a decision, the more people will resist using evidence to make it.

It's an interesting hypothesis. On the surface, Lovaglia's Law seems somewhat absurd, as one would think that the reliance upon empirical evidence would increase commensurate with the importance of a decision. However, upon reflection, we can think of countless examples of large personal and business purchases that have been rationalized. Did the buyer really need that Rolex or that Porsche?

People have an innate need to appear logical to others. Having said that, buyers often make emotional decisions and then back into the reasons. Assume that you're at a party, and you see a guest that you don't know arrive in a Mercedes 600S. When you meet that person, you mention that you admired his car and ask how he came to choose that particular model. Because you don't know each other very well, the reasons offered will almost certainly be logical: safety, resale, reliability, and so on. Had you known this person better, the real reason might have surfaced: "I look a lot handsomer in this car than I did in the Buick I was driving!" This emotional buying decision can be justified to others (and sometimes to the buyer himself) with logical reasons.

Robert Sutton is a professor of management science and engineering at Stanford Engineering School who, along with Jeffrey Pfeffer, coauthored the book *Hard Facts, Dangerous Half-Truths and Total Nonsense*. Sutton wrote:

> *Clearly, the more important the decision, the more people involved stand to lose and gain, and the more strongly they push for outcomes that enhance their self-interest rather than are best for everyone involved.*

While logic and hard facts play a role in the buying process, it seems clear that emotions and rationalization are important factors as well.

What is the buyer seeking at this phase of the buying cycle? The buyer is seeking assurance or, put another way, confidence. The buyer "needs" the confidence to proceed to the final step, and confidence is an emotion. As a result, confidence evolves from a B2B buyer's belief that the purchase will empower her to achieve a goal, solve a problem, or satisfy a need and that others will perceive it as having been a good decision. The question that a selling organization has to worry about is how the buyer develops this confidence, and how the seller can ensure that the buyer develops confidence in its solution.

Timing versus Urgency

Fairly early in a B2B buying cycle, the buyer becomes aware of a need and its importance. In some decisions, the importance of timing weighs more heavily than the importance of fully addressing the need itself. In other cases, the importance of the need outweighs the timing, as there is a lower sense of urgency. For an example of timing being more important, think back to 1999, when corporate procrastinators had to scramble to find Y2K fixes. Viewers of the movie *Office Space* can comically relive this experience, but at the time, companies were panicking to ensure that they had a fix for the Y2K bug.

The bug was a programming issue involving the date field on computer databases, particularly accounting and customer databases. Software developers weren't sure that their previous versions would function properly once the calendar rolled to the year 2000—hence the urgent need to have a solution prior to 12/31/99. It was less urgent that the new application or patch go through normal rigorous testing in other areas, but it was critical that the patch was in place in time.

Y2K created another phenomenon: it made selling technology far easier in the late 1990s. First of all, excess hardware and software was purchased in anticipation of potential glitches. We believe that, even more significantly, "no decision" virtually disappeared from the buying landscape. Being Y2K compatible wasn't optional. Ironically, laggard (late market) buyers often drive salespeople to distraction because deferring the decision is a frequent outcome. If three vendors bid on the Y2K job, it was nearly a certainty that one of them would be awarded the transaction. It is unlikely that this situation will recur anytime soon.

Other examples across industries where timing may take precedence over functionality for a particular need include a solution enabling companies to accelerate time to market, a hospital that has unexpectedly lost its backup generators as a result of a natural disaster, and a start-up company that has had the good fortune to land a big client and the misfortune to have a nonrecoverable server crash the day before implementation.

Now, contrast the Y2K example with this. Consider a business that has grown over the past five years from a one-person start-up to 400 employees today, operating in six countries. Despite its apparent success, the firm is still using the same desktop accounting system that it has used from the start. This hasn't been a problem for most of the company's existence. The accounting was relatively simple, and the application handled general ledger, accounts payable, and accounts receivable just fine. Payroll was outsourced to a third-party firm.

As the company expanded throughout Europe from its U.S. headquarters, it began experiencing needs that the initial system couldn't accommodate, such as the need for

- Multiple, simultaneous users via a Web portal

- Higher levels of data security

- Invoicing in multiple currencies at local levels and the ability to convert currencies to the U.S. dollar at the corporate level for reporting

- Custom, ad-hoc reporting

- Budgeting at a business unit level, with roll-ups to regions and corporate

While the need for an improved solution was important and the executives (and auditors) were pushing for a solution quickly, this was clearly an important, long-term decision that needed careful consideration. It was important to "get it right." Thus, a buying committee was formed with representation from all internal and external user groups across countries. In the end, the CFO would be responsible for the recommendation to the board of directors, but many other people would play an important role in the process. For example, beyond the normal functional requirements a CFO would want in an accounting system, the CEO is positioning the company for an IPO or to be acquired. In either scenario, value will be increased if the company's accounting system, accounting records, and audit trail are consistent with what is expected for public company scrutiny. So the CEO cares that the system works as it should, but he also has a preference for solutions that can inspire confidence in investors.

Therefore, the importance of the actual need outweighed the importance of the timing. This led to a very detailed definition of requirements, a thorough search process, and a methodical search for reassurance.

These examples illustrate the seesaw effect of the roles that timing and need play in the buying process, and have inspired the authors of this book to offer our own law to describe it:

> *Law of Buyer's Assurance: The more urgent the timing of a purchase, the less assurance will be required by the buyer in advance of the purchase. The more urgent the need for the purchase, the more assurance will be required by the buyer in advance of the purchase.*

It is critical that sellers and marketers understand the Law of Buyer's Assurance if they are to navigate the buying cycle successfully. By fully understanding where the buyer is sitting on the assurance seesaw, the seller can determine whether he has an opportunity to accelerate the decision time frame or whether he should be more sensitive to fully meeting the buyer's need for assurance that this is the right solution for her. Sellers very often make a misstep here, which helps to explain why they are often trying to close transactions that aren't yet closable. The buyer isn't ready.

Researching Reassurance

Former U.S. President Ronald Reagan was fond of using the expression "trust, but verify." Typically he would use this phrase in the context of discussing relations with the former Soviet Union, but we suspect that if Reagan were a procurement officer for a corporation, he would once again utter those words during Stage 4 of the B2B buying cycle.

Prior to social networking, reassurances were most effective when the salesperson wasn't involved. A buyer's first choice would be to talk to customer references that were in a similar business and had implemented the same offering. Third-party consultants and white papers were another way to gain confidence in the decision. Rather than talk with the seller, potential buyers would be more comfortable talking with support staff from the vendor.

This book is focused on changes in buyer behavior as a result of technology and the Internet. So, how have these advances affected the buyer who is at Stage 4 of the buying cycle? The primary answer is social networking, which has given the buyer immediate access to, often, an unlimited number of people who can affect the buyer's level of knowledge and, ultimately, her confidence that the decisions she has made are best for her.

Consider a report authored by Forrester Group in February 2009 titled "The Social Technographics of B2B Buyers." The report revealed the findings of an online survey of 1,217 North American and European decision makers at B2B firms with 100 or more employees, and it is among the first research available that profiles the social behavior of business buyers (see Figure 6-1).

Some highlights from this research include the following:

- A full 91 percent of these technology decision makers were "spectators" overall, with 69 percent reporting that they were active spectators for business purposes. The fact that they are spectators means that they are reading blogs, watching videos and Webinars, reading white papers, and using other forms of social media.

- Some 55 percent of responding decision makers were members of social networks, referred to as "joiners" by Forrester.

- Some 43 percent of respondents were creating media, such as maintaining blogs, uploading videos or articles, and so on.

- Finally, 58 percent were "critics," reacting to content that they see in social networking environments such as blogs and newsgroups. As such, their comments are likely to influence buyers at various stages of the buying cycle who happen to stumble across their contributions.

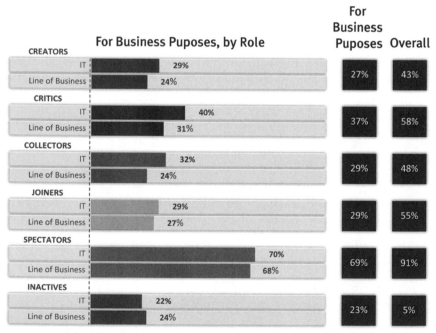

Base: 1,217 North American and European technology decision-makers at firms with 100 or more employees

Figure 6-1 *The Social Technographics Profile of Technology Decision Makers*

Source: Forrester Research, Inc., **The Social Technographics® of Business Buyers.**

In addition to the Forrester study, Nielsen BuzzMetric released an intriguing research report in early 2009 called "Global Faces and Networked Places." Among the results, the report found that although the total amount of time spent online increased by 18 percent in 2008, the amount of time spent on member communities rose by 63 percent!

These data and others clearly indicate that technology has changed buyer behavior and allowed buyers to express their need for social interaction within business environments. Social networking and blogging sites are now the fourth most popular Internet activity, behind search, portals, and software applications. In addition, time spent on social network and blogging sites has grown at more than three times the rate of overall Internet growth!

It's not just happening in the United States; it's happening everywhere. It's not just personal use; it's business users too. And it's occurring across all age groups. For example, the Nielsen study claimed that "the greatest growth for Facebook has come from people aged 35-49 years of age (+24.1 million). Furthermore, Facebook has added almost twice as many 50-64 year old visitors (+13.6 million) than it has added under 18 year old visitors (+7.3 million)."

Driving Influences for Reassurance

Whether it happens over the course of several weeks, months, or years, the B2B buying cycle has a number of checkpoints that must be passed. If they are not passed satisfactorily, the buyer does not receive $200, does not pass go, and makes no purchase. Sometimes these checkpoints are somewhat informal, as in the case of newer or smaller companies that have yet to establish more formal procurement procedures. In the case of larger, more established companies, the roadblocks can be quite trying. In either environment, the person making the buying decision may or may not have a lot to gain by making the right decision, but he'll certainly have a lot to lose by making the wrong one. So the pressure to be sure—to be right—weighs heavily upon the buyer's personal shoulders.

The need for reassurance goes under many names in the B2B buying cycle. Whether it's referred to as a cost versus benefit analysis, an ROI analysis, or a plain old "sanity check," there is a definite need to know—to have confidence—that the best purchasing decision is being made. Larger companies like to "help" ensure that employees make sound purchasing decisions by having a proof step. Often this goes by the name of

- Cost versus benefit analysis

- ROI analysis

- Expected rate of return

- Impact analysis

- Sanity check

Part of getting comfortable with a buying decision is doing a financial analysis of the cost versus benefit of the offering being considered. This is an important step not only in verifying that value will be realized but also in trying to secure funding.

Salespeople who believe that they are competing only with other vendors in their space are sadly mistaken. They don't understand the fierce competition within organizations for funding new initiatives. Assume for a moment that a CFO has five different requests, each for $100,000, to fund new projects, but can approve only three of them. It is likely that her decision will be made based upon which three of the requests offer the highest returns on investment. This also highlights the fact that those projects with a calculated cost versus benefit stand a better chance of being approved.

In such a case, three salespeople will get good news that will result in orders. The other two will be informed that their projects have been put on hold, but the reality is that they lost, either because they hadn't helped the client do a cost versus benefit calculation or because their payback wasn't as attractive as it needed to be.

Another aspect of competition for funds occurs when unbudgeted initiatives are introduced. Budgets are put in place to control spending and with the objective of being able to meet earnings expectations. Few companies enjoy the luxury of being able to simply increase spending if new requirements arise. You need to be a government to do that! The most common way to find budget is by reallocating money. If the new initiative is believed to deliver a greater payback, others that don't measure up can be eliminated. Once again, unfortunate salespeople will be told that their proposals have been deferred until next year, when in reality they lost to a vendor selling a completely different type of offering.

Fighting for Funding

In doing a financial analysis, buyers need to know the following variables:

• Total costs

• Total potential savings

• The timing of both costs and savings

In the interest of avoiding a discussion of net present value calculations, let's focus on the first two items, but recognize that the lower the up-front investment and the sooner the benefits start, the better the return. In the software industry, the advent of software as a service (SaaS) has dramatically improved returns on investment by minimizing start-up costs while accelerating implementation times.

Buyers want to know all the costs associated with the offerings they buy. The costs they would want to include go well beyond the price of the offering itself and include items such as

• Sales tax

• Shipping costs

- Installation costs

- Infrastructure needed to support the implementation

- Professional services

- Ongoing maintenance and repair

When vendors omit some of these costs, they compromise the validity of their analysis. Buyers should be fully aware of the costs going in and hate "surprises" once projects are under way.

As you can imagine, estimating cost is far easier than determining potential value or benefit. Understanding buyer skepticism, vendors face a choice:

1. They can provide their value proposition, but they run the risk of buyers either discounting it or not buying in because it comes from a vendor or seller who is trying to justify and finalize a sale.

2. Guide buyers into providing their own estimates of potential savings. One approach is to establish baselines for several areas of potential improvement and have the buyer be responsible for deciding how much (figure or percentage) value could be provided. It is helpful to have either documented results of other clients or industry averages to help guide the buyer in establishing estimates of value.

Our preference is to take the latter approach. We (and many buyers) have come to despise vendor "value propositions," which are usually generic statements describing potential paybacks. By this time, we hope you agree that telling a buyer how good it's going to be amounts to selling rather than empowering buying. Buyers have come to believe that value propositions represent the highest possible benefit that can be realized. As a result, most of them will reduce their expectations significantly when attempting to quantify value in a cost versus benefit analysis.

In trying to quantify value during sales calls, it may be appropriate to ask a buyer how much improvement is possible. Often, however, to give a reasonable answer, a buyer will need to have proof, potentially via a reference account that provides an idea of what results are possible. For any intangible or complex offering, until proof is provided, sellers are asking buyers to trust that the offering will work as advertised and deliver results. As mentioned previously, buyers at this stage are in a "trust, but verify" state of mind.

Vendors will also find that some additional work prior to implementation can provide significant benefits. Late in the buying cycle, vendors and buyers can agree on measurable metrics that are expected to improve. It is important that vendors choose variables that they exert a high degree of control over. For example, for vendors selling CRM, increases in the top line would be a dangerous metric because even if the vendor met all expectations, the client's revenue can be adversely affected by the economy, a competitive offering, quality problems, and so on.

For CRM, it may be appropriate to measure win rates on proposals because managers would have electronic access to qualify or disqualify opportunities and prevent sellers from issuing proposals too soon or, worse yet, to unqualified prospects. This is a metric that should improve regardless of outside variables.

Vendors that take the time to go through these extra steps of measuring results gain four advantages:

1. When a new client is near the end of a buying cycle and is going through the risk phase, the thought that a vendor will monitor results on an ongoing basis tends to be reassuring to buyers.

2. When a vendor uses existing clients for proof, prospects expect them to say glowing things about the offering, support, service, and so on. However, if a customer can also provide tangible business results, it goes a long way toward helping the prospect envision that this payback can be achieved.

3. Having a prospect decide how much a particular metric can be improved can be challenging. If, however, the seller can reference

actual results of a client in a similar space, it is easier to quantify potential value. For example if a CRM buyer is having trouble deciding how much improvement there can be in win rates on proposals, a seller would have the option of citing that the ABC Company increased its win rate from 15 percent to 23 percent. At that point, the seller can ask what the prospect feels is possible and is likely to give a midrange figure.

4. In the case of social networking, where vendors exert minimal control over customer opinions, it stands to reason that buyers with measurable results are more likely to give strong recommendations. If they can cite actual results in numbers or percentages, the person asking for input is likely to be impressed.

While customer reference accounts are vital and are a primary source of information in gaining a level of comfort that a vendor will provide a positive experience, there are other areas that a salesperson should consider:

• Vendor stability is important, especially if your company is a start-up or smaller company. Over the years, many buyers have gone with stable companies (IBM, Microsoft, Intel, and so on) based more upon safety than upon functionality.

• Professional services is an area where almost every salesperson assures prospects that his company hires only "the best and the brightest." If you are going to assign a project leader or primary contact, consider introducing that person to the buyer, or at a minimum provide a summary of previous projects she's worked on that are similar to the proposed engagement.

• Customer service and customer support are areas that can also provide a competitive advantage, but can be difficult for a seller to convey. If doing a reference call or visit, the seller may want to ask the customer to spend some time discussing his experience with the vendor in these areas.

Reassurance is an important step for a prospect who is trying to get comfortable with making a vendor decision. As we've discussed, it is an area that goes beyond the offering, so try to be sure to cover as many bases as possible. Prospects will appreciate sellers that rely on customer testimonials and resist efforts to tell them how good it's going to be.

The Sales Plan: Positioning Yourself to Win the Reassurance Phase

So, what does all this mean for B2B marketers and sellers? For one thing, it means that B2B buyers are highly socially active and, whether you like it or not, are getting most of their information from sources that you do not directly control. Regardless of your industry, if you don't have a marketing and sales plan that includes social marketing, you're late to the dance. Not too late, but you may want to get going and consider an ongoing plan to be everywhere your prospects are.

In addition, this means that you (as a salesperson or marketer) and your company should consider changing the way you sell, with the goal of understanding the stages of buying cycles and facilitating buying. The language and approaches of the past are not relevant in the new age, and, as Darwin suggested, those who are most fit are the ones who will survive and flourish. It's time to adapt.

Here are a few ways that can help you and your company to succeed in Stage 4 of the buying cycle.

1. A simple but powerful way in which B2B marketers and sellers can participate in social media is to answer relevant questions on sites such as LinkedIn, Yahoo! Answers, and others. According to the Small Business Search Marketing blog, Yahoo! Answers, Answers.Com, and About.com collectively received more than 169 million search click-throughs in December 2008. Along with the data from Forrester, this strongly suggests that prospects are online and asking questions. They are seeking information that will give

them confidence. These questions can be answered by anyone, but if your company has a strategy to search for and respond to these questions, you have a great opportunity to gain influence over buying decisions.

2. Adopt a marketing culture that understands that buyers will pass through this stage. In doing so, marketing programs can implement lead-scoring models that detect what stage a buyer is in, and tailor communication to be appropriate for the buyer at that stage. As an example, if you know that a prospect is being managed by an assigned sales rep and, based on feedback from sales, the prospect is now in the reassurance stage, you can develop sales support materials that help the prospect to determine ROI or value.

3. Adopt a sales culture that understands that buyers will pass through this stage. As we mentioned earlier, many salespeople have been trained to sell rather than to empower buyers. It is the buyer's job at this stage, not yours, to seek whatever he needs to become reassured. You should anticipate this need and be prepared to help him find the reassurance he's looking for. Don't make the mistake of assuming that the buyer will skip this stage and just sign the agreement. Like the couple that lingers in the house without the Realtor while approaching the buying decision, the prospect will need to consider everything he's learned so that he can decide whether or not to move forward. If you've adopted a sales culture that understands that this will happen, you will have quietly provided all of the information that he's likely to need at key points of the buying cycle.

4. Finally, assign someone on your staff to constantly scan all online sources of information that your prospects may be looking at. By doing so, your reconnaissance person can provide insight into what is being said, good or bad, about both your company and your competitors. Use this information to anticipate what your buyer may be thinking or feeling, and be prepared to offer reassurance. If you find posts about your company online, participate

in the discussion in a positive, constructive way. This is particularly necessary if there are negative or derogatory posts about you, as there almost certainly will be from time to time. Even the largest, most successful companies endure negative attacks. It doesn't stop them from framing the conversation to focus on their perspective, often positioning themselves in a positive light and having the effect of reassuring the readers. You can do the same.

Summary

Reassurance is a necessary step for buyers, largely based upon the history and stereotype of sellers and vendors hyping their offerings. Sellers must be patient with buyers during this stage and not merely view it as something that stands in the way of receiving an order.

Rather than being offering-intensive, the buyer's focus is more along the lines of verifying the type of results that can be achieved through using the offerings, along with how the offerings can be implemented and supported. During the reassurance stage, sellers that refrain from sharing their opinions or trying to impose them on buyers will be in better alignment. The most effective type of information that sellers can provide during this stage is actual results that their customers have achieved, either through success stories or by allowing prospects to contact customers.

STAGE 5: RISK–THE GO/NO-GO BUYING DECISION

The rehearsal dinner was a huge success. Friends and family members shared stories and toasts, expressing their heartfelt happiness and best wishes for the couple to be married the next day. At 9:30 the bride and groom say good night. The next time they'll see each other will be tomorrow at 1 p.m., dressed in their formal wear at the ceremony, when they will be asked to commit "'til death do us part."

Neither of them sleeps especially well, as both are burdened by the realization that this is one of the most important decisions they will make in their lives. Committing to each other, buying a home, hopefully raising a family, and working to have a comfortable retirement lie on the horizon as both comforting and frightening prospects. They attempt to envision what their lives will be like 10, 20, and 30 years or more in the future. Thoughts of couples who were just as happy when they got married but who for some reason weren't compatible surface. If the bride or groom has divorced parents, she or he attempts to figure out why things went awry for them. There is an urgent need to feel that everything will be okay and that this is the right decision.

Brief thoughts of panic arise, followed by concerns about whether the potential mate is absolutely the right one. While extreme, the question of whether waiting a few more months would help to further solidify the choice arises. Traits in the other that each wishes could or will change over time come to mind. An uncomfortable amount of time is spent pondering things that could go wrong in a marriage with *the* person that each has chosen out of all the people he or she has met during adult life. Relationships and potential conflicts with future in-laws are also a source of concern.

The overwhelming majority of couples successfully navigate through this risk phase, which is part of how human beings make decisions. The doubts that are raised and considered are somehow overcome, but virtually everyone feels pressure when he has to make a final decision and commitment. The fact is that with 100 or more people gathered, the facility rented, meals arranged, and other preparations made, it would be an especially difficult and painful decision to elect to back out of at the eleventh hour. Deciding not to finalize a "buying" decision has far fewer implications.

B2B Buying Decisions

While we don't want to be overdramatic, there are some common human emotions that almost invariably arise just prior to making important choices. During many sales or buying cycles, the "courtship" with the salesperson continues smoothly until buyers have to make a decision and ultimately spend money. Few salespeople are fully aware of the thought processes and emotions that buyers go through at the end of a buying cycle. Before making any major decision, it is normal human behavior to question whether now is really the right time to make a commitment. Understanding buyer emotions and aligning with them can be the difference between winning and losing a sale (be it to another vendor or to no decision). It is a time when traditional selling behaviors (addressing objections, pressuring, and closing) can make the decision to buy more difficult. Buyers can either decide not to move forward or choose to delay (make no decision).

Let's examine some of the dynamics that occur at the end of a fairly lengthy buying cycle.

After considering five different vendors for electronic content management (ECM) software, a clear choice has emerged for your health-care company. As the VP of patient services, you recognize that the current paper-based system requires costly storage space, makes retrieval and refiling a labor-intensive process, makes the cost and turnaround of reproducing and distributing documents prohibitive, and makes full HIPAA compliance virtually impossible. Insanity is doing the same thing repeatedly and expecting a different result. Replacing physical documents with scanned electronic images and electronic key word search capability is the only way things will improve.

You have received buy-in from your CFO, your CIO, the director of records, and the call center manager, but this project clearly has your fingerprints all over it. You've championed the idea of leveraging the technology to reduce costs while improving productivity and compliance. As with any work flow application, several areas within your organization will be involved. Many of the people in the affected departments will be skeptical and will not welcome change with open arms. Your expectation is that some staff members will openly resist change. To realize the projected benefits, it will be necessary to get buy-in from all the managers, who will then be responsible for driving user acceptance. Given your 11 years with the company, the visibility of this project has the potential to move your career path ahead by being a gateway to other opportunities and promotions. You also realize that anything less than a successful implementation could end up being a career-limiting decision.

The vendor you've chosen provides what the committee (and you) feels is the best overall fit in the key areas that have been identified:

- The vendor is a stable, financially sound organization.

- It has extensive experience in working with health-care companies.

- It has a large regional office with support personnel within 50 miles of your main location.

- Its offering is proven and provides the major capabilities needed.

- It has a large and experienced professional services staff.

- The lead support person has implemented the system for two local health-care organizations.

- The salesperson has been competent and professional, and you feel that he will do a good job of overseeing the implementation and ensuring that the necessary support resources will be provided.

- Several contacts from reference accounts gave the vendor high marks.

- Independent consulting companies have given favorable reports.

Despite the thoroughness of the evaluation, there is a knot in your stomach when you consider what you have riding on this decision and, most importantly, the implementation.

You call George, the salesperson you've worked with over the last five months, and request a meeting in your office. During the last meeting you had with him, the final proposal was presented, and it accurately summarized the organization's needs. You couldn't hide your excitement about how the ECM system could transform your organization. It was time to move into the twenty-first century by completely changing document workflow.

Buyer Behavior Changes with Risk

When George arrives, he notices your somber mood, which is in stark contrast to the upbeat tone of your last meeting. After a terse introduction devoid of small talk, you begin by telling George that you want to share concerns you have about the decision that is on your plate. You proceed to express the doubts that you have about moving ahead with the project:

- Potential user rejection of the new approach.

- IT's ability to integrate legacy applications with the new software.

- IT's ability to adhere to the implementation schedule. Any slips will adversely affect the anticipated payback.

- When new technology might make the software you are buying obsolete.

- Extensive up-front costs, especially in light of the current economy.

- The significant capital investment that is necessary.

Maybe the decision should be put on hold for a while.

This appears to be horrible news for a salesperson who has five months of effort invested, is under pressure to make his numbers, and has committed in his latest forecast that this opportunity will close within 30 days. The litany of concerns could make it appear unlikely that the sale will happen.

Fortunately, George has the wisdom to realize that these risk objections are strong indicators that his company is the vendor of choice. A less experienced seller might have interpreted them as indications that she was losing. In drawing this incorrect conclusion, the salesperson might have made the potentially fatal mistake of dropping price. If a buyer is sharing concerns relating to risk, there are a few critical things that sellers should know:

1. Only Column A (the vendor of choice) earns the privilege of seeing a buyer express risk concerns. It actually means that the transaction is George's to win or lose. Risk concerns arise when a buyer imagines how the implementation will proceed and what could potentially go wrong. This happens only when the buyer is envisioning what will happen after the purchase is made. This is a stressful and unpleasant exercise that, ironically, the buyer will go through *only with the vendor that she believes is the best alternative.*

2. Discounting in response to buyer risk concerns is like pouring gasoline on a smoldering fire. The message that George would send by discounting is that the concerns about risk are valid. Many sellers wrongly assume that the buyer's decision will be made easier by making the offering less expensive. Clearly, in this ECM decision, the buyer's concerns are focused on implementation success and visibility. If the cost were too high, the buyer would never have advanced this far in the buying process. Price isn't the issue at this point. George's best course of action is to attempt to help the buyer overcome the risk concerns. If and when these concerns are overcome, it is likely that George will be pressured for a better price prior to finalizing the sale. After overcoming risk, in a buyer's mind, cost changes to price, and the concern becomes getting the best possible deal.

3. There are many risk objections that George would not be able to address in a credible manner. Virtually all of these *objections are based more in emotion than in logic.* Consider the areas of concern mentioned. With the exception of IT issues (assuming that George has professional services and resources to offer), any attempt to address them would amount to the seller trying to tell the buyer why she shouldn't be concerned. Not many sellers will be successful in convincing buyers that they are wrong to feel the way they do.

4. Recognize that risk is an emotional hurdle for a buyer. After discussing those issues that appear addressable, George should attempt to calm things down by acknowledging that this is an important decision and making the transition from emotional concerns to the logic behind the effort both organizations have expended in this evaluation. George's best course of action would be to summarize the potential value, the shortcomings of the current manual system, the capabilities needed, and the references that have been provided, and then gently ask the buyer to move forward.

When a buyer displays risk concerns, it is critical that the seller remain calm (something that is not easy to do when a large order appears to be slipping away), fight any inclination to offer pricing concessions, and avoid exerting pressure by closing. At this stage, a salesperson has earned the business but must be patient in allowing the buyer to attempt to work through her issues. Sharing risk concerns means that the buyer is comfortable enough with a salesperson to vent. That salesperson is the vendor of choice in almost all cases. Many times in our lives, when people vent, they are not looking for someone to resolve their issues; rather, they want to be heard and are looking for empathy with their situation. Venting is usually done only with people who are trusted. People who vent are seldom seeking advice (unless it is consistent with the direction in which they are already leaning).

If and when a buyer overcomes risk concerns (either during the meeting or at a later time), a curious shift in behavior takes place. Once a buyer makes the decision that the potential upside of ECM outweighs the risk, as shown in the buying curves model, price becomes the issue at hand. In Phases 1 and 2, the quotation is viewed as being cost. When making a purchase decision, however, cost changes to price. Another way to look at it is that to continue through the buying process, a decision had to be made that the buyer could afford the ECM system. Knowing that sellers "leave room" in quotes (similar to the sticker price on a car) means that the focus now becomes whether the buyer is getting the best possible deal.

Buyers would be remiss if they didn't complain that a vendor's price is too high. Such requests almost invariably put sellers on the defensive. Many respond by asking the *most expensive six-word question* in the selling profession: "Where do I need to be?" This surrenders control to the buyer, who can logically assume that by asking this question, the seller not only has acknowledged that a discount is appropriate, but also has great flexibility with regard to price. The worst outcome is having a buyer take this opportunity to suggest a ridiculously low number. This figure will be less than what the buyer is willing to pay. Consider how the final negotiated price will be influenced by the initial figure the buyer requests.

Smart buyers have been taught how to arm themselves for negotiations. They are told to get at least three bids and try not to let vendors know if they're winning or losing. Price negotiations should begin in reverse preference order, starting with a request for a "best and final" number from Column C. That figure is used as leverage to get a "best and final" bid from Column B and ultimately a discounted number from Column A.

It is not unheard of for buyers to fabricate numbers. After the years of perceived abuses that buyers have endured, would they lose any sleep over lying to a salesperson? They're likely to come home that day and during dinner gloat to their spouse that they actually manipulated a salesperson!

Just as George had to be calm and professional to try to help the buyer overcome risk concerns, the same is true with requests for discounts. Buyers like to perpetuate the myth that price is the biggest variable in making buying decisions. That may be true when making commodity decisions, but think about the ECM decision. The CFO, CIO, director of records, and call center manager have all been involved and have expressed preferences. Choosing a vendor has far-reaching implications for the organization. If price were the primary factor in making a decision, Procurement would be able to choose the vendor.

One of the reasons that price is perceived as being such a critical decision criterion is that it is the most common excuse given to the Columns B and C vendors when they are told that they didn't get the business. In most cases, buyers realize that those sellers have spent time and effort competing. Coming in second doesn't pay very well. Buyers have to deliver unwelcome and unpleasant news to salespeople who lose, and therefore they look for the easiest way to let them down. Blaming product is one way (although that really means that it was not really a qualified opportunity), but it can lead to discussions that can get heated. The tried-and-true best way out for a buyer is to say something like: "This was a hard decision, and I'm sorry to have to tell you that we awarded the business to another vendor who had a slightly lower price. We appreciate your efforts and will keep you in mind for any future requirements." When vendors compete, only one gets the order. Every other seller (unless she was incompetent or obnoxious) is told that she came in second. The real reason the vendor lost hardly ever shows up in a loss report: it got outsold!

This approach allows sellers B and C to maintain their dignity and dutifully check "price" on the loss report. Let's step back for a minute, however. If the buyer really wanted to do business with either of them (had one of them been the vendor of choice), wouldn't that vendor have been given an opportunity to sharpen his pencil and make the sale? For that reason, we believe that the only time price is a valid reason for a loss is if a seller was asked to, but could not, match or beat a competitive quote.

Human Buying Behavior

Throughout the book, we've highlighted the ways in which buyers have leveraged technology to change the way they determine their needs and evaluate their options. While these tasks can be accomplished with minimal involvement from salespeople, assessing risk and negotiating price still net out to predictable human behavior that hasn't changed appreciably over the last 50 years.

A phenomenon that many of our clients have experienced over the years is a large percentage of opportunities that result in buyers deciding not to decide. We refer to these as losses to NDI (No Decision, Inc.). For most companies, losses to NDI occur more frequently than losses to all of their named competitors combined. We hope that having a better understanding of buyer behavior can help you better align with buyers as they are making a decision, and we would like to offer reasons why NDI is such a formidable competitor.

For transactions of any consequence, risk assessment takes place just prior to making a buying decision. In the example of ECM used in this chapter, there are different types of risk for the various committee members:

- The CFO's concerns may focus on the return on investment relative to those for other initiatives that are being considered.

- The CIO is likely to be worried about the resources and time needed to make the implementation schedule.

- The director of records may be concerned that the new approach will reduce her head count and therefore her position within the organization.

- As director of patient services, and the person who drove the evaluation of ECM, you have the largest-scale concern for the overall success of the project and its implications for your position within your organization. Without necessarily stating this as fact, other committee members have delegated responsibility for the overall success of the project to you. If things do not go well, you may feel like a pincushion as others lay blame on you rather than accept responsibility by virtue of participating in the decision process.

Traditional selling approaches view risk concerns as a fundamental human reluctance to spend money. We hope you realize that they are more complex than that. There is another subtle but significant aspect of empowering buyers rather than selling them. It is a matter of responsibility and control. Without malice or bad intent, the vast majority of salespeople and vendors assume ownership of the final result. In the case of ECM, here are some typical seller statements:

- "We'll reduce your document management costs."

- "Our software will eliminate HIPAA violations."

- "ECM Inc. will improve patient satisfaction."

Vendors make "value propositions" in advertising and on their Web sites in the same fashion. Even if buyers don't fully believe them, we've all come to tolerate these statements, but there is a fundamental issue with them, and it has to do with who is ultimately responsible for achieving these results. It may surprise you to realize that ECM software and most other B2B offerings don't, can't, and won't do any of these things, nor can the seller, support people, or the vendor. The buyer has to implement the software, drive user acceptance, and ultimately own the achievement of the desired business results.

Human beings have an innate need to exert control over their personal and business lives. When assessing the risk in making an ECM software decision, you would probably try to imagine things that can go wrong, what action could be taken in response, and who would take that action. How comfortable would you be with the assumption that the seller, software, or vendor is going to reduce your costs? Buyers are left to make this leap of faith when they are "sold" in the traditional manner.

Empowered buyers understand that vendors merely provide capabilities that they or their staff must implement and use to achieve the desired business outcome. Buyers that accept responsibility for the final result are much better prepared to consider and overcome concerns about risk when finalizing a buying decision. At this point, assurances by sellers to unempowered buyers that everything will be fine ring hollow and may even compromise credibility.

Further complicating matters is that when they see buyer risk concerns, sellers may misread them as a sign that the sale is slipping away, either to NDI or to a competitor. Their most common response will be closing or discounting techniques. Either can be detrimental. When a buyer is looking at risk, pressure by a seller can make no decision the most attractive alternative. Offering a discount validates the buyer's concern about risk.

Ironically, if a seller sees risk concerns near the end of a buying cycle, she actually has earned the business. The challenge is to display empathy and patience. Those qualities are in short supply for many sellers in the best of circumstances. When they've been working on a sale for a long period of time, it is extremely difficult for them not to continue to close the buyer. Of course, when a buyer feels pressured, it means there is much more selling than buying taking place.

Doomed Proposals

Suppose for a moment that two months into your evaluation of an ECM system, a friend asked when you felt your decision would be finalized. Let's also suppose that your friend could ask the salesperson working on the account when the order was closable. Guess whose date will most often be earlier? Most people believe that the seller will be more optimistic about when the order can be closed. Consider that when a buyer is asked for an order before he is ready to buy, he will feel pressured. The best outcome is usually that the order is closed, but discounting was necessary to give the buyer an incentive. The worst case is that the seller's attempt to close offends the buyer, so that an otherwise successful end to a buying cycle has been lost.

In our experience, the majority of closing on B2B transactions is being done based on the seller's agenda. Often, senior management sets an expectation that revenue must be realized this month, this quarter, or before year end, although these dates have little or nothing to do with when the buyer will be ready to commit. Contributing to this may be that sellers often write proposals prematurely. Selling organizations seem to feel that writing a proposal is a step toward getting an order.

Consider the ECM example used in this chapter and what information you would require before you felt you were in a position to choose a specific vendor and purchase its software. Here is a potential list of what you would need to know:

- The business issues you are trying to address with ECM

- Business issues that other members of the buying committee want to address

- The shortcomings of the way you currently handle documents

- The capabilities needed to achieve the desired results

- Detailed activities needed to implement the system

- Detailed work flow using the new system

- The IT effort required to integrate ECM with your legacy applications

- Professional services that vendors or outside consultants must provide

- Training needed for IT and end users

- The cost

- Which vendor provides the best alternative

- Estimated cost versus benefit of implementing ECM

- Proof that vendors can provide what they claim to offer

- Financials so that you can verify that your vendor is viable

- Backup and disaster recovery procedures

- Whether you are getting the best price possible

Unless and until you have all these details covered, regardless of the vendor's desire to book the order, any attempt to close would be premature. Another way of looking at this is to conclude that all of these details must be determined before the seller issues a proposal if that proposal is to serve as a vehicle for a buying decision. In the best of circumstances, a proposal (especially multiple copies to members of the buying committee) is a poor way to ask for an order. If copies of a proposal are delivered to five committee members on March 24, how likely is it that the decision will be made by the end of the first quarter? Once a proposal is more than about a week old, the Column A vendor often finds that buyers will not take her calls. They have everything they need in terms of information, and they know that if they take a seller's call, they will be asked if a decision has been made.

How often do salespeople manage to be in front of decision makers at the end of buying cycles to ask for orders? Failing to orchestrate this access often leads to attempts to close people who are not authorized to make decisions. Several potential issues can arise:

- You exert pressure in asking the person to commit for the organization.

- Even if the person agrees that he would like to do business with you, he is not authorized to do so.

- The buyer may begin to negotiate a lower price, and then the seller is told to meet with the decision maker, with the discounted price serving as a starting point for further negotiation.

To our way of thinking, *closing is the logical conclusion of a buying cycle that should make sense for both buyer and vendor.* We often hear sales executives comment that their people "are not strong closers." Such statements may reflect a lack of selling skills throughout the buying cycle! If a seller has done a poor job throughout, it is unlikely that superior closing skills will carry the day against competent sellers.

Summary

As you have seen throughout the book, technology has empowered buyers to significantly change the way they buy. Overcoming risk concerns and making commitments will continue to evolve over time, but they have been minimally affected over the last several years. What has changed is that risk assessment can now be done via social networking if the buyer enjoys the luxury of knowing one or more people that went through making a similar decision.

Vendors that provide high-quality offerings, support, and service stand to benefit from this word-of-mouth feedback. To take it a step further, vendors that can quantify the results of implementing offerings empower their customers to do a better job of giving referrals, as those referrals will contain measurable results.

At the end of a buying cycle, the buyer is concerned about whether she is making the right decision, whether vendor commitments will be honored, and whether she will ultimately realize the desired results. During this risk stage, the seller's role is more being a sympathetic ear than attempting to talk a buyer through risk concerns. When the conversation shifts to price, the buyer has overcome risk and now wants to be sure that she is getting the best possible deal.

PART 3

Fostering a Sales Culture That Facilitates Buying

HOW TRADITIONAL SELLING CONFLICTS WITH THE NEW BUYING PROCESS

Now that you are aware of the five stages that buyers go through, we'd like to highlight areas where traditional selling conflicts with what buyers want and need from sales organizations. Vendors that fail to recognize and remedy such situations will be unable to provide a consistent buying experience that otherwise could become a competitive advantage. As you'll see, organizational changes are necessary to better support individual salespeople.

Old habits die hard. Buyers have long memories of unpleasant experiences with salespeople for valid reasons. The generally accepted notion that sales is about convincing, persuading, and overcoming objections sets the stage for confrontation rather than collaboration when buyers and sellers interact. Selling is perceived as something that is done to, not for or with, buyers. There are several reasons for this widespread opinion and many culpable parties, so in pointing out contributing factors, there is no shortage of blame to pass around.

While they represent a fairly small percentage of the total, negative encounters with B2C sellers shape buyers' opinions long before B2B buying takes place. The obnoxious car salesperson sets the bar low for all others. Early, crude, repetitive attempts to close or qualify exert unwanted pressure on car buyers. Many people cringe when they hear questions like

- Do you prefer the silver one or the blue one?

- Will you be trading a car in?

- Will you be leasing or buying?

- What do I have to do to put you into this car today?

These questions pressure buyers. The seller adheres to the stereotype by trying to move the buyer in the direction in which he'd like the buyer to go, and the buying experience suffers as a result.

Car salespeople have very short-term objectives. B2B vendors have monthly, quarterly, and annual pressure to achieve top-line revenues that filter down to sellers. Deadlines can cause B2B salespeople to misbehave, sometimes at the direction of their management team: "Do whatever you have to, Joe, but don't come back without the order!" These imposed deadlines have little to do with when buyers want to finalize their decisions. Closing is most often done according to sellers' or vendors' agendas.

Wall Street contributes to the problem by insisting on quarterly guidance for earnings. If a vendor recognizes revenue on a $5 million order on April 6 rather than March 31, should its stock valuation be significantly different? To the investor community, the answer is a resounding yes, but when you step back, this doesn't make a tremendous amount of sense. These quarter- or year-end pressures bring out the worst behavior in selling organizations, often including discounts or other incentives that erode margins.

As specified by the Constitution of the United States, in the eyes of our legal system, people are presumed innocent until they are proven guilty. That seems to apply to everyone except people whose titles have anything to do with selling. In such cases, Napoleonic law applies. Salespeople are presumed guilty (of all the horrible things that previous sellers have done to buyers) unless and until they prove themselves different from the stereotype.

This feeling about salespeople is nearly universal. The only exceptions we've seen are in Eastern bloc countries, where mothers would love to have their sons or daughters aspire to become salespeople because the profession pays well and is held in high esteem. The underlying difference is that there is no residual negative baggage. Under communist rule, there was no free trade, and therefore there were no salespeople to abuse buyers and shape their opinions.

At some level, vendors tacitly acknowledge that the negative stereotype exists. When you look at business cards, it seems as if the human resources staff has gone to a thesaurus in search of misleading, euphemistic titles such as account executive, marketing representative, regional manager, industry specialist, and so on. How often have you seen "salesperson" used on a business card? Do vendors really think they're fooling buyers by avoiding use of the "S" word?

Vendors further reinforce the negative stereotype by knowingly or unknowingly accepting the traditional definition and perception of selling within their organizations. The vast majority adheres to the standard definition by default. In doing so, they turn a blind eye to the fundamental human need to exert some control over sales calls when interacting with salespeople.

Albert Einstein is credited with saying that insanity is doing the same thing over and over and expecting different results. Control equates to being allowed or, better yet, empowered to buy. Selling is an attempt to control buyers.

Sales training programs contribute to the problem. Many of them espouse methods for manipulating buyers. Such techniques fail to treat buyers as human beings, instead viewing them more as laboratory rats that will react in a desired manner if a technique is properly applied. Consider how we've all come to accept the fact that sellers are expected to try to overcome objections. The most common approach is the dreaded "feel, felt, found" approach, where a seller empathizes and then tries to get past an objection by presenting a contrary perspective: "I understand how you feel. Others have felt the same way, but they found that. . . . " Buyers often have valid objections. Such objections cannot (and should not) be overcome or handled. Is it realistic to expect buyers to change their minds because they are told they are wrong to feel the way they do? Buyer objections are a reality. Hopefully, a seller has other areas of strength that can allow the buyer to make a favorable decision. However, it is possible that the objections being offered are valid and that the seller's offering is not a good fit for a given buyer.

Many closing techniques are used so commonly they've been given names, such as the

- Puppy dog close

- Assumptive close

- Eight yeses close

- ABC

- Trial close

- Limited-time offer

- Red light/green light close

- Ben Franklin close

A recent Google search on "sales closing techniques" returned 321,000 results! If you look at some of the descriptions of these techniques, you will find words and phrases like *clever stunt, secret, a few tiny adjustments, assume your customer is going to buy, change what others think, overcome any objection, killer rebuttals,* and so on. After reading them, you feel as though you want to shower!

These selling techniques show a total lack of respect for buyers as individuals. There is an emphasis on manipulation and closing. These techniques don't allow for any possibility that a purchase may not make sense for a buyer or that a seller's offering may not fit a particular buyer's needs. The common *Glengarry Glen Ross* phrase "Always be closing" shows a total disregard for buyers and fails to recognize that premature closing exerts pressure on buyers.

We've also heard many senior executives bemoan the fact that their salespeople are "not good closers." It doesn't occur to them that their staff members may not be good salespeople. If someone were to write a terrible three-act play, even the best writer in the world could not craft a final scene that would salvage it. In our experience, having a buyer purchase is the culmination of a buying cycle in which the seller has done a professional job throughout.

The best salespeople often don't have to close. If they are patient and cover all the bases, there are times when buyers volunteer to buy. If a buyer can articulate her goals, the reasons she can't achieve them, the capabilities needed, proof, an implementation plan if appropriate, the value, and the price, the decision to purchase is a logical conclusion.

Another issue is whom the salesperson is closing. Unless he can get in front of the decision maker, asking someone to commit when she is unable to do so is demeaning and puts pressure on that person. Finding a way to talk with the decision maker when a seller has earned the right to close has a great impact on the likelihood of a favorable outcome.

While we're on the subject of closing, one of the absolute worst ways for salespeople to ask for the business is via proposals. Many sales organizations view the proposal step as progress in moving the sales cycle forward. For that reason, proposals are issued prematurely (before all the details that a buyer needs in order to make a decision have been defined). Curious things happen once a proposal is issued (especially when multiple copies are sent to all committee members):

- There is a nearly guaranteed delay of two to four weeks before a decision is made, as, supposedly, everyone has to review his copy, hold hands, look skyward, and agree on which vendor to choose.

- Many proposals are thick enough to serve as alternatives for prescriptions for sleeping disorders. How many proposals have you seen that a senior executive would never take the time to read?

- Within a week, phone calls from salespeople remain unanswered. Buyers know why they are being called and either haven't made a decision and don't want to be pressured or have made an unfavorable decision and don't want to break the news to the seller.

- For every week the proposal sits, the chances that the seller will ultimately get the business wane. It is frightening to see pipelines with proposals that are two, three, or four or more months old, yet still remain at 90 percent probabilities in the forecast.

Professor of Sales

Colleges and universities have been painfully slow to recognize sales as a profession. Graduates today are prepared for careers in accounting, engineering, teaching, and other fields. Despite great demand, however, there aren't many graduates who are ready for a career in sales. Compounding the issue, companies today don't offer the lengthy training periods that were common in the 1970s at organizations like IBM and Xerox. The good news is that over the last 15 years or so, the number of schools offering undergraduate degrees in selling has increased about fivefold, but there is still a long way to go to give credibility and substance to a career that is in demand in both good and bad times for competent salespeople. Despite the progress that is being made, our concern is that many universities place the emphasis on traditional selling rather than on empowering people to buy. It would be a huge step in changing the buyer-seller dynamic if 22-year-olds had a definition and approach to support the way buyers want to buy.

The characteristics required to achieve at high levels in sales are daunting: strong verbal and written communication skills, ability to handle rejection, willingness to be paid based upon production, above-average IQ, and so on. We suspect you know doctors, lawyers, or engineers who are highly competent, but who would fail miserably in sales. Despite this, the profession is low on the ladder of career choices. Validation with formal degrees would go a long way toward changing attitudes.

Training Produces "Wind-Up" Toys

Executives are unwilling to tolerate "spray and pray" sales calls, and yet product training points salespeople in that direction. Vendors treat product training and sales training as separate silos. Sales calls should be about the buyer's situation first, but it takes an exceptional salesperson to be able to know how to do that after completing whatever product and sales training a vendor provides.

Many salespeople simultaneously covet and dread gaining an audience with a senior executive decision maker. Such calls have to have a positive outcome. If these calls are neutral or negative, the seller would have had a better chance if she had relied on internal champions to sell the senior executive.

It takes an extraordinary salesperson to be able to attend product training and then distill the germane information needed to call on a particular title within a vertical market for a specific offering. According to Sales Benchmark Index, 13 percent of salespeople generate 87 percent of the revenue. This leads us to believe that extraordinary sellers are in very short supply.

Traditional product training treats offerings as though they were nouns. Sellers learn multitudes of esoteric facts about "it." Given a choice, executives would prefer not to be educated on such facts. Rather than having them be inanimate objects, vendors give offerings a life of their own with statements such as

- "Our CRM system will drive higher revenues."

- "ECM will reduce document management costs."

- "Our billing system will reduce your receivables."

The truth is that this is yet another case of vendor hype, as offerings are incapable of producing business results. Rather than focusing on nouns, sellers would be better served in executive calls by being prepared to convey what an executive's staff can do by using their offering to achieve business results.

Ultimately, executives don't want to read (or be read) the entire novel. They want the "Cliff Notes" version: a 30-minutes-or-less call that lets them understand the usage of offerings at a high level. If they are interested, they will delegate understanding all the necessary details (reading the novel) to lower levels that include actual users of the offering.

A Lack of Coordination

Vendors view product development, product marketing, and sales as three separate entities and fail to define "touch points" that describe how these groups should interact. Especially in large organizations, product development and product marketing may be far removed from the ultimate users and therefore run the risk of operating in a vacuum.

We've seen many product development people take the attitude: "If we build it, they will buy." Questioning a product architect about who would buy a new offering and how she would justify it can elicit sighs or outright scorn. The easiest approach to having a successful new product launch is to have that offering contain functionality that fits the needs of the market, yet many companies don't have a good way to ensure that this happens.

Let's assume that product development has a new offering that fails to address the needs of the marketplace. Once its development efforts are completed, it charges marketing with creating campaigns and collateral to drive demand. Ultimately, when the product is launched, marketing is expected to support sales in its efforts to find new customers for this offering.

As you can see, this procedure is more product-centric than customer-centric, but it happens in vendors that view product development, product marketing, and sales as separate silos.

Failure to get product development and marketing on the same page manifests itself where the rubber meets the road: at the salesperson level. After going through whatever sales training and product training is available, sellers decide on an individual basis how to position offerings by the words they use in talking to buyers. The task of positioning offerings never appears in a seller's job description, nor does it belong there, but dysfunctional coordination between silos places this burden on each salesperson. Only about 10 percent of sellers are capable of successfully accomplishing this task, and often only within vertical segments where they have extensive experience.

One startling example of poor communication happened at an account we worked with years ago. The company sold a $35,000 software package that was used to help manufacturing companies minimize unscheduled downtime. The original software was written in DOS, and as time went by, the VP of sales saw the lack of Windows support as an increasingly common reason given on loss reports. We believe that the most common reason for a loss is being outsold, but salespeople usually list price or product (it couldn't be that they are incompetent).

Finally the company decided to invest the money needed to develop and release the Windows version while phasing out support for DOS. Within three months of taking that action, guess what began to appear on the loss reports? The lack of DOS support! Companies without a common process and vocabulary trying to develop products based upon loss reports are like a person trying to drive a car by looking in the rearview mirror.

When you examine behavior at an individual or organizational level, there are two reasons that desired changes don't occur. The person or organization

- Cannot accomplish a task (skill deficiency).

- Will not accomplish a task (motivational issue).

Sadly, few vendors over the last 40 years have had the knowledge and the desire to fundamentally change the manner in which their sellers interact with buyers. This represents a lost opportunity, and such organizations should be concerned now that buyers have started to take matters into their own hands. We are hopeful that the motivational issue for vendors will become far more compelling, and we believe it will. Vendors that find ways to align with the newly empowered buyers will prosper. Those that stand on the sidelines of this revolution put their revenue stream at risk.

By leveraging technology, buyers have spoken loud and clear in creating a road map for how they want to be treated. These changes are long overdue, and it is unfortunate that buyers have had to lead the way. They have the luxury of speaking with their corporate checkbooks, and they will favor vendors and sellers that provide superior buying experiences by aligning with the way they want to buy.

Let's Make a Deal

Implementing changes in the way an organization and its salespeople sell is a significant challenge. It requires a structure that gets development, marketing, and sales on the same page. We'd like to suggest some changes in the vocabulary used within vendor organizations:

- Eliminate the use of the word *deal*, not only when talking with buyers, but also when having internal discussions. B2B "deals" don't give anyone the feeling that the sale is anything more than another notch in the seller's belt. A suggested alternative is to substitute the word *transaction*, both internally and externally.

- Eliminate the use of the phrase *sales cycle*. By this time, we hope the reason should be clear in that the focus of this term is inward- rather than outward-looking. Using the term *buying cycle* at least has everyone within a vendor organization looking in the right direction: toward the buyer.

- Refrain from using the term *buyer objection*. The knee-jerk reaction is that objections can and should be handled or overcome. Recognize that your offering may have some shortcomings in the buyer's eyes. Our suggestion is to use the term *buyer concern* and to recognize that some concerns are valid and cannot be overcome.

- When forecasting, do not focus on when your organization feels a transaction can be closed; rather, choose an estimated date when a client or prospect will be ready to buy.

   Other implementable suggestions are:

- Take a fresh look at your SFA or CRM milestones. In our mind, these systems are not at all customer-centric. One of the first steps in implementing these systems is to define your sales cycle. According to Bob Schmonsees, author of *The Black Hole*, over 90 percent of vendors never take how their buyers buy into consideration when defining their milestones.

- If your company has multiple types of sales, such as add-on business, professional services, renewals, and small, midsize, and large transactions, consider defining separate milestones for each (taking into account how people buy, of course). It stands to reason that the larger the transaction, the more steps there will be in measuring progress. One size does not fit all.

- Try to ensure that when you issue proposals, they contain all the components the buying committee needs in order to make a decision. Don't confuse an initial quote with a proposal. Sellers have a tendency to want to issue proposals early because they see it as a step in moving the process forward. In doing so, they run the risk of having proposals sit for a long time.

- Managers should project one sell cycle ahead to ensure that sellers have adequate activity in their pipelines to meet their quota. Most CRM or SFA systems can capture close rates for individual reps at each milestone, apply them, and project future revenue. This enables mangers to be more proactive rather than reactive. A healthy pipeline also minimizes those quarter ends where vendors are scrambling, discounting, and pressuring buyers to make revenue targets.

Summary

There are innumerable books giving approaches and advice for improving interpersonal relations. In terms of sheer numbers, the buyer-seller relation has to represent the largest pool of people where things could be improved. All of us are buyers that interact with salespeople.

We view selling as a wonderful way to make a living, and we recognize that to excel at it takes a fairly extraordinary skill set. The often-heard opinion that someone "has a nice way with people" and therefore would make a good salesperson is incredibly naïve and fails to recognize what it takes to be a competent B2B seller.

Consider two scenarios in which you are the buyer:

Seller 1 enters the initial call with a desire to convince or persuade you to buy a particular offering.

Seller 2 enters the call with the initial objective of learning what you know about the offering to be discussed; letting you share a goal, problem, or need that you have; and determining if he can provide you with the capabilities necessary to empower you to achieve the desired results.

We hope you conclude that Seller 2 would provide a superior buying experience. With everything being equal (the offerings and prices), Seller 2 will win the business more often than not. Aligning with customer buying cycles requires changing the mission and perception of selling.

GETTING PRODUCT MARKETING RIGHT

Nearly every salesperson will acknowledge that leading with product is a cardinal sin in selling. Mentioning product too soon leads to premature price discussions. Without a sense of potential value, any price will seem high to the buyer if it is given too early. With that as a backdrop, could vendors have chosen a worse term than *product marketing* for such an important function? It has been a poor choice for several reasons:

- It smacks of the traditional definition of selling.

- Having *product* as the first word fosters inward rather than outward views and perspectives.

- There is no mention of the buyer or the target audience.

- There is no mention of usage, potential buyer benefit, or buyer experience.

From a vendor perspective, the goal has been to promote and sell products and/or services, hence the term *product marketing*. There is nothing wrong with this goal, and indeed a vendor wouldn't exist for long if it were unable to consistently sell enough of its products to remain viable. The real problem is the cultural consequences of this term, as it initiates a chain of thinking that is internal rather than external, such as employees focusing on the

- Need to sell $X product this quarter in order to hit *their* goal.

- Features of the product that they can emphasize so that customers will be intrigued.

For these reasons, we believe that product marketing is an unfortunate name. Perhaps vendors would fare better with the term *customer solution marketing*, or CSM if you prefer an acronym. Whether your offering is a product or a service, the inherent meaning behind CSM is that the focus is on customers and the solutions to whatever need, problem, or goal they have that they can achieve through the use of the offering. This, of course, requires an understanding of the buyer's needs, problems, and goals, which should foster a different kind of thinking in the marketing and sales continuum.

Consider the implications of this simple change for the hiring process. If you are recruiting a product marketing manager, the interview conversation will naturally focus on the need for the applicant to sell product. This will be translated into goals, such as market penetration, number of new product sales, revenue goals, and so on.

Conversely, if you are recruiting for a customer solution marketing manager, the conversation will turn to how she will go about understanding customer needs and how she will match those needs to the solutions you offer. This too will translate into goals, which should include vendor revenue goals. However, the focus will shift to understanding the difference between the means and the end. The end is the revenue goal. The means to achieving that goal becomes establishing two-way dialogues with customers so that their needs, problems, and goals are fully understood. Those needs are factored into the feedback cycle for tailoring the solution, and the emphasis is on matching customers with the solution that will best help them.

Considering how redefining this role can affect interviewing for the position starts to provide an understanding of the significant changes that can result. Executed properly (top-down), this change permeates the organizational culture and aligns with the buying process. The focus becomes outside in and enables vendors to stop thinking of themselves as sales organizations and start viewing themselves as buying facilitators—an army of employees prepared for the mission of understanding their customers' needs and helping them to buy.

How Did We Get Here?

The seeds for making selling difficult can be sown by the founders of start-up companies or the architects of new offerings for established companies well before an offering is turned over to product marketing. These creative people have concepts that they feel should be developed and brought to market. The founders of companies or architects of new offerings face additional challenges if they are closer to being engineers than to being salespeople. Often product architects are familiar with the technology needed to develop their solution, but are equally unfamiliar with the needs of the customers that would buy and use their offerings. Their primary concerns center on the shortcomings of what's available in the market from a product standpoint, and this can cause them to miss the forest for the trees. Customer requirements should be the focus, yet few organizations create environments in which that is part of the culture. The easiest way to sell an offering is to have it be something that buyers want to buy. If you doubt this, look no further than the turmoil American auto manufacturers faced in 2009.

Toward that end, developing offerings without first defining the vertical segments that hold the greatest potential is a major gaffe. Taking this a step further, clarity can be achieved by attempting to identify the targeted titles within those segments, and business issues can be addressed to more than offset the investment in the new offering. The more compelling the business case, the easier it will be for buyers to justify choosing the offerings.

These steps are relatively simple, yet common sense is a resource that is in short supply. Venture capital companies fall into the same trap when they invest in start-ups. They place a great deal of emphasis on the track record of the "jockey" (aka the CEO) and the offering itself, yet they decide to make multimillion-dollar investments by looking at pie charts showing market potential. People seeking funding nod and wink (trust us) and tell potential investors that after acquiring the first few customers (how?), they will be able to go from zero to 8 percent of the market within four years (how?).

Every projected revenue chart for a start-up looks exactly the same. Revenue figures start at zero and begin a steady, unrelenting climb upward for the first five years. Have you ever seen a revenue projection from a start-up that shows a downturn in year three or four?

Beyond the five-year revenue ascent, presumably, the future is too cloudy for the founders to see what will transpire. Yet they can see the first five years clearly. And thus begins the subconscious culture of driving sales and product so that the market penetration and revenue predictions are realized.

Some founders or product architects are highly offended if they are asked for details as to how top-line revenues will be achieved. They appear to have accepted the mantra: "If you build it, they will come!" A healthier approach for everyone involved in product design and development would be: "If we build it, who will buy it and why?"

If a new product offers continuous improvement, founders or product architects look at the cost, specifications, and overall performance of what is currently available and incorporate what they feel are advantages. In such cases, the good news is that there is a market that has already been established, so putting together a marketing/selling plan is fairly straightforward.

For offerings with no comparable counterparts, the challenge is far greater. There are two major types of innovation for new offerings.

New Variations on Old Themes

One form of innovation is developing an alternative to existing offerings with a dramatically different business model. Saleforce.com (SFDC) is viewed as the company that pioneered the software as a service (SaaS) concept that has become commonplace. In its case, a number of vendors had established momentum for customer relationship management (CRM) software, albeit with some drawbacks:

1. Significant up-front costs not only for the software, but also for IT and professional services expenses that were required to tailor the system so that it dovetailed with the sales environment and other applications. Many of these costs had to be amortized over five years or more, meaning that there was a relatively long-term commitment to whatever software was chosen.

2. Delays in realizing benefits because of the amount of time required to fully implement all modules.

3. The cost of ongoing maintenance to provide support and receive new releases of the software as they became available.

4. Virtually no ability to scale down in the event of a reduction in the number of people needing access to the system. Lifetime "seats" were purchased up front.

5. Changing vendors was a major decision, given that all of the up-front costs and customization related to the initial installation would have to be replicated. Even if "better" offerings were available, companies deferred moving to them until the initial investment had been written off.

Despite all these disadvantages of traditional CRM, SFDC faced an uphill battle at first, especially when selling to larger companies. Aided by the traditional CRM vendors, prospects raised objections:

1. Data security, as all of the sales pipeline and sales information was stored by the vendor. Any breach could have catastrophic consequences.

2. Less functionality than the legacy systems in the marketplace.

3. Limited ability to modify the software.

4. For early buyers, the risk that the market would not embrace the new concept and that SaaS would ultimately not be a viable business model.

Salesforce.com was able to get buyers to see that the benefits of its approach outweighed these concerns. Its strategy for entering a space that was already established and offering a different business model was, in retrospect, brilliant. Previous CRM market leaders such as Siebel were slow to react and defended their installed customer base model. As a result, Salesforce.com grew exponentially, and its success has dramatically shifted how software is purchased.

SaaS provides a more predictable revenue stream, but the customer base of vendors is more at risk, given the relative ease of making changes. It places a premium on setting realistic expectations and making sure that results are monitored so that customers realize the benefit of continuing to remain as customers.

Disruptive Offerings

As witnessed by the outsourcing of jobs starting in the late 1990s, the cost of doing business in North America is a competitive disadvantage for vendors, especially those that manufacture a product. One of the real strengths of the American economy is the ability of entrepreneurs to develop offerings that open entirely new markets. Such offerings are referred to as being disruptive, meaning that there are no directly comparable offerings.

While exciting, the challenges of bringing such offerings to the market are daunting. Consider the pie chart we showed in Chapter 3, which is repeated in Figure 9-1.

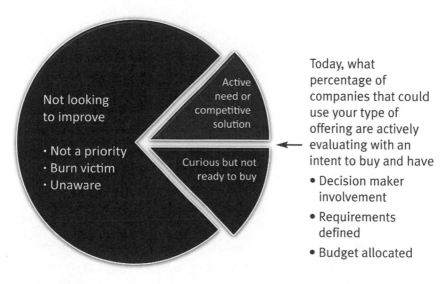

Figure 9-1

By definition, nobody is looking for offerings that are entirely new concepts. At the start, there aren't even any people who are curious! Therefore, 100 percent of the demand must be proactively generated. This is a marketing challenge that isn't for beginners or for the faint of heart! Most of the early accounts have to be acquired by selling one at a time, often with the full support of the executives of the start-up.

As Geoffrey Moore has pointed out in several books, early market buyers (innovators and early adopters) have the ability to find emerging technologies. These are bright people who can see new offerings and envision how they can use them (create an application for them). There have been instances where these buyers have "bailed out" vendors who suddenly are shown a defined market segment to pursue. When they are ready to ship a disruptive offering is one of the rare instances in which vendors can be successful by leading with product to attract early market buyers.

The good news is that some of these early market buyers will find you and buy. Additional good news is that you'll find that the buying cycles of the early market are fairly short. If the buyer is going to gain a competitive advantage by being first, it doesn't make sense to spend a year making a buying decision. The bad news is that

- There aren't enough early market buyers to meet revenue projections (they make up only 5 to 20 percent of the total).

- Early market buyers share some unique characteristics:

    They will endure a "spray and pray" by a founder or salesperson to gain an understanding of what capabilities are provided.

    They determine specific areas of their businesses where the offering can be applied to realize a return on their investment.

    Early market buyers are risk takers and don't need the assurance of a large customer list (there isn't one), a company with a 30-year track record, a strong balance sheet, and so on. These buyers make bets on innovation and recognize that some buying decisions will not deliver the desired results. Better to make some bold decisions than to wait until "safe" decisions can be made several months or years later in the product cycle.

If a seller or founder doesn't fully understand where and how an offering can be used, there can be no manipulation. Stated another way, early market buyers buy; they are not usually sold.

Formalizing a Sales Organization

After receiving funding, 10 "beachhead" accounts have been closed, most of them with heavy involvement by the cofounders of the organization. The investors want to see revenue growth and make it clear to the CEO/founder that it will be necessary for her to hire a professional VP of sales and that it should be someone with substantial experience. That requirement makes the CEO realize that there are no viable internal candidates and a search will have to begin.

In her personal and professional life, the CEO has had negative experiences with salespeople and therefore does her own stereotyping of salespeople and selling. She lacks a formal sales background and has mixed feelings about hiring a sales executive:

• Sales is a necessary function, but her preference would be for the firm's offering to be so superior that buyers would flock to her doorstep.

• She hasn't been overly impressed by the salespeople involved in securing the initial accounts. They helped the firm get in the door, watched as others did the heavy lifting in building the business case and credibility needed, and then seemed to negotiate final pricing more on behalf of the prospect than of the organization that they worked for.

• There is a great deal riding on generating top-line revenue. Finding someone to delegate that task to would free up the CEO to focus on the aspects of the business that she prefers, primarily continuing to develop the offering.

- Despite all its efforts to date, the firm's success or failure will be determined by whether or not it can drive the top line. It will be difficult for her to manage a VP of sales, given her limited knowledge of selling.

There have been many references to salespeople and sales executives as being gunslingers for hire. The CEO has built a culture that she is proud of that puts customers first and attracts qualified people that fit in. It is clear that anyone who is hired to run sales will come in with his own ideas, and that the sales organization is likely to be a separate ecosystem that will be shaped in the way the new VP wants. The CEO's concern is that revenue and commissions will trump her priority of taking care of customers.

Once a start-up company or a new offering has begun to gain traction and acceptance, the potential vertical markets and applications are known. The highly skilled, intuitive sellers that joined the company because of its attractive compensation plan and stock options have gotten it to a critical point, because now the drill is to begin to tap into the mainstream market (which represents 80 to 95 percent of the total potential for the offering). Many of these salespeople accepted promotions to sales managers/executives based solely upon revenue production and without regard for what type of manager they will make. Some people feel that the skill set needed to be an individual contributor is dramatically different from the skills needed to assess, develop, and drive revenue through salespeople that are a cut below the first ones that joined the company.

For many vendors, bad things begin to happen at this point, and traditional selling (with every negative consequence possible) becomes the vehicle used to drive the revenue engine. Buyers beware! Without giving it a great deal of thought, most of the "beachhead" clients endured a founder or salesperson leading with product, but they were smart enough to figure out where and how the offering could be used.

The sellers who helped establish the critical mass of customers had virtually no support from the company in terms of how to position offerings and what vertical segments to focus on, but somehow they were able to get things done. The latest batch of new hires needs help and direction, so marketing prepares collateral and presentations to drive late market buyers toward making buying decisions.

To illustrate the challenge of selling to the mainstream market more clearly, we'd like to combine the research done by Sales Benchmark Index with the statistics that Geoffrey Moore provides. On the left side of Figure 9-2, you'll see the 20 percent who are early market buyers (which may be on the high side for many offerings) and the 80 percent who are mainstream market buyers. By doing some math, you can determine how often the two different buyers will be called on by the two categories of sellers. For example, in the upper left quadrant, the decimal equivalent of 13 percent times 20 percent yields a figure of 2.6 percent. That means that given these assumptions, 2.6 percent of the time, an A player will be calling on an early market buyer. A players are effective in all selling situations, so the vendor has a reasonable chance of success.

Continuing the calculations, 17.4 percent of the time, a B/C player will be calling on an early market buyer. While at first this may seem undesirable, early market buyers will sit through spray and pray sales calls and are capable of visualizing how an offering can be used. This is a rare case in which leading with product may be successful. The focus of the early market buyer is much more on the qualities of the offering rather than on the selling skills of the salespeople. Early market buyers buy (they aren't sold), so this situation will still give the vendor a reasonable chance of a purchase being made.

The lower left quadrant indicates that 10.4 percent of the time, A players will be calling on mainstream market buyers. This is the best use of A players because they have the patience to first discuss a buyer's potential needs, are able to focus on business issues, and can relate product usage.

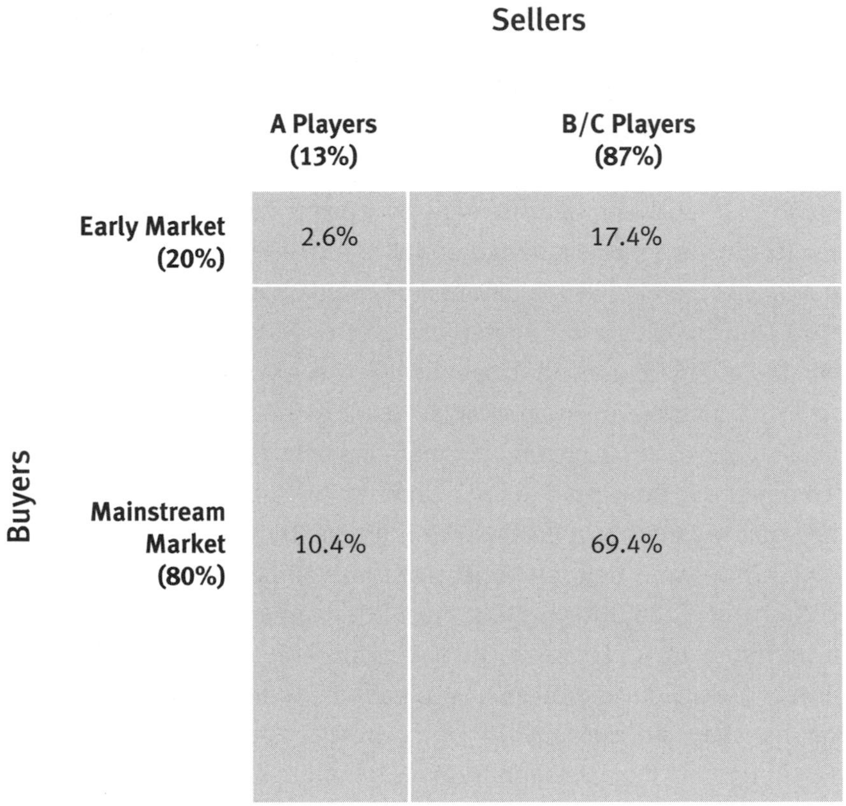

Sellers

	A Players (13%)	B/C Players (87%)
Early Market (20%)	2.6%	17.4%
Mainstream Market (80%)	10.4%	69.4%

Buyers (vertical label)

Figure 9-2

The lower right quadrant shows the real issue that growing or mainstream organizations face. About 70 percent of the time, B/C players who lead with product and are most comfortable calling lower in organizations are calling on mainstream market buyers who are struggling to understand how an offering will be used. These sellers may have been successful with the early market, as they were riding the wave of an innovative offering that gained acceptance from early market buyers. As soon as the early market begins to dry up, revenue production from B/C players will wane.

The senior executives of a company may get a false sense of sales success during the early market stage of rolling out a new offering. They had salespeople and marketing collateral that led with product. As a start-up begins to grow its sales staff, the attractive stock options are no longer available, so a lower percentage of A players will join. The majority of the calls these new hires will make will be on mainstream market buyers.

These less talented salespeople go through product training and are turned loose on their assigned territories. They focus on

- Selling rather than empowering buyers

- Product rather than first understanding the buyer's current mode of operation

Predictably, buyers recognize the sellers' attempts to convince, persuade, handle objections, and so on. If the buyer has done some research using the Internet (as some buzz is generated), these salespeople drift even further out of alignment. The shame of it is that companies that are searching for the holy grail of having a sustainable competitive advantage soon find that price and product aren't the answer. The fact is that if price and product are relatively equal, the better salesperson wins. Aligning with how people buy and redefining selling is one of the few differentiators with staying power. Sellers need help in getting there, and it has to begin with customer solution marketing (formerly product marketing) getting it right.

Customer Experience Management (CEM)

One of Steven Covey's most frequently cited quotes is: "Start with the end in mind." We'd like to offer a different approach to customer solution marketing that focuses on the ultimate customer buying experience. While some B2C companies have been successful in doing this, we are unaware of any B2B companies that make the buying experience a competitive advantage across the board.

In order to do so, product development, product marketing, tactical marketing, and sales have to be on the same page. We'd like to propose an approach that lays the necessary foundation for that to happen.

The Foundation for the Process

As dysfunctional as they may sometimes be, product development, marketing, and sales exist for the same reason: top-line revenue. Despite their common objective, however, they typically lack the functional links that would enable them to coordinate their efforts. We'd like to propose a structure that will change that by integrating those silos and providing a single lens through which to view potential customers. The vehicle we propose organizations can use is Sales Ready Messaging, and we want to provide a high-level overview of how it can be created.

Ideally during, but in the worst case after, product development, an attempt should be made to define the vertical markets and the titles of the people who would be involved in making a buying decision for each offering. Given that many people in product development are more engineers than salespeople, this could (and should) be a joint effort among all three groups. Certainly it would be a red flag if no vertical markets and applications could be identified, as the organization would be running the risk of announcing offerings in search of markets.

After identifying vertical markets and titles, we suggest creating a Targeted Conversation List (TCL) that goes a step further (see Figure 9-3 for an example of a TCL). For each title, identify a menu of business objectives (goals) that buyers are likely to have and that the offering can help them address. In B2B situations, these goals should be ones that buyers are willing to spend money to achieve. This exer-

Targeted Conversation List Example

CFO[S,F]
forecasts

Achieve profit projections with accurate sales
Reduce the cost of sales
Align sales and marketing efforts

VP of Sales[S,I]

Improve forecasting accuracy
Shorten start-up time for new sales reps
Achieve revenue targets
Increase cross-selling revenue

VP of
Marketing[S,I]

Lower the cost of distributing and tracking leads
Improve close rates on leads

CIO[I]

Support implementation with limited resources
Secure customer/pipeline data from competition

[S] Sell
[F] Fund
[I] Implement (conversion/compliance)

Figure 9-3 *Targeted Conversation List Example*

cise in creating a TCL amounts to a sanity check on whether an offering has an identified target audience.

Once customer solution marketing, marketing communications, and sales agree on the TCL for each vertical market, they have a basis for communicating with one another. The TCL also allows marketing to aim its curiosity and interest generation efforts using a rifle rather than a shotgun. Efforts with collateral, trade shows, Webinars, Web sites, advertising, and so on, will be geared toward the agreed-upon vertical markets, titles, and business issues in the TCL.

Before an offering is released to the field, a more detailed step should be taken by CSM, marketing communications, and sales, and that is to drill down and map the capabilities of the offering for each title/goal combination in the TCL. This is a step that is usually abdicated to salespeople, who may or may not realize, after the traditional product training they have received, that in sales calls at high levels, they should be discussing only *relevant* features or capabilities. This step also minimizes spray and pray calls and means that the major objective in a call with a buyer is to have him share one or more goals from the TCL.

CSM, marketing, communications, and sales have an annoying habit of using feature names and acronyms that executives don't readily understand. A major misalignment takes place if and when sellers use such terms. Often buyers won't ask for clarification, but the use of these terms can cause confusion and make the buying experience far less than optimal. For that reason, we suggest converting features into *usage scenarios* that will make it clear how a buyer could use them. The four components of a usage scenario are

- **Event.** What could happen during a business day that could trigger a need for the feature within the buyer's organization.

- **Question.** In hoping to empower buyers, it is much more powerful to ask rather than to tell. Asking questions also allows the seller to know what the buyer wants.

- **Player.** Who (in some cases what) will respond to the event.

- **Action.** Describe at a conceptual level how the offering will be used to address the event.

For example, a feature of CRM would be to create standard pipeline milestones, but merely mentioning that feature leaves a lot up to the buyer to determine how these milestones could be used or could be beneficial. A usage scenario can make things clearer:

- **Event.** After making calls, . . .

- **Question.** . . . could your pipeline be more accurate if . . .

- **Player.** . . . your salespeople . . .

- **Action.** . . . . were prompted to update a central database via laptop to reflect progress made against predefined standard milestones?

  If a buyer answers yes to a usage scenario, two things become clear to the seller:

- The buyer understands how the feature can be used.

- The buyer agrees that she wants or needs the feature.

After mapping all features to a buyer (vertical market and title) for a specific goal, converting them to usage scenarios, and sequencing them, a questioning template can be created that would help a seller have a conversation with a high-level buyer about a goal that the buyer wants to achieve. This document, however, is far more than a template in that

- It provides consistent positioning of offerings that eliminates features that aren't relevant to achieving the business goal.

- It should represent best practices for all offerings and vertical markets.

- It allows organizations to have average sellers emulate the calls that their best salespeople would make.

- It frames or defines the outcome of a sales call, as the buyer's "solution" has to be some subset of the usage scenarios.

Because sellers shouldn't lead with product, the last step in creating a template is to write packets of diagnostic questions that a seller should ask to determine which usage scenarios a buyer is likely to need. This means that there is a one-to-one mapping of diagnostic questions to usage scenarios. By posing the indicated usage scenarios as yes/no questions, the seller understands which ones the buyer wants. The final question of need development then becomes: "If you had (summary of usage scenarios that the buyer agreed to), then could you achieve (the goal)?" If a buyer says yes, she is empowered to achieve the results she wants.

Each title/goal on the TCL becomes a conversation that should be mapped out for salespeople. Figure 9-4 is an example of a prompter that would be used to make a call on a VP of sales who wants to drive higher revenue with a CRM system.

If you take a close look at the prompter in Figure 9-4, you will notice that with the exception of the header information (Title, goal,

Title: VP Sales
Goal: Achieve revenue targets
Offering: CRM

What barriers to achieving your revenue targets exist today?

Topic 1: Update opportunity status daily against milestones

How do managers keep current with the status of opportunities? How often do they get updated by their reps? How do they get updated? Have you established milestones to gauge progress?

Topic 2: Protection of data when territory changes take place

How do reps review past activity when assigned new accounts? How available and useful is documentation? Between new hires and turnover, how many reps per year are added? Does a lack of continuity ever cost you business?

Topic 3: Plan activity levels based upon historical close rates

How do managers determine if reps have enough activity to achieve quota? Do reps stop prospecting when their funnel looks healthy? Do some have peaks and valleys due to this trend? How do sales managers monitor activity to ensure that quotas will be met? Do they adjust for varying close rates of reps? How?

Topic 4: Bottlenecks identified and flagged for managers

How do managers identify bottlenecks in a rep's pipeline? How many deals are lost because opportunities stall? If aware of a bottleneck, would managers offer suggestions to move opportunities forward? How would they do it?

Recap: *"So your current situation is. . ."*

and offering), all the printed information is in the form of questions. As stated earlier in the book, buyers want to exert some control over where a sales call goes. By asking questions, the seller goes in whatever direction the buyer takes him without offering opinions or trying

Figure 9-4 *Solution Development Prompter*

What capabilities are you looking for to help you achieve your revenue targets?

Event:	After making calls could your pipeline be more accurate
Question:	if your salespeople were prompted to update a central
Player:	data base via laptop to reflect progress made against
Action:	predefined standard milestones?

Event:	When assigned new territories could start-up times be
Question:	reduced If salespeople (or new hires) could access a
Player:	password-protected database and review activity in their
Action:	accounts over the last several months?

Event:	When reviewing activities could sales managers be more
Question:	proactive with their reps if the system applied historical
Player:	close rates to each stage of a rep's pipeline and
Action:	highlighted those whose activity will yield below-quota performance?

Event:	When time thresholds are exceeded for a milestone
Question:	could stalled opportunities be reduced if the system
Player:	alerted managers and prompted them to e-mail
Action:	suggestions or contact the salesperson to brainstorm strategies or approaches?

Confirm solution: *"If you had (capabilities) could you achieve your revenue targets?"*

to tell the buyer what she needs. This provides a positive buying experience that is devoid of attempts at manipulation.

As a result of creating and agreeing to a TCL, it is much easier to coordinate marketing and sales efforts because the target audience has been identified. Thus, a lead can now be defined using the TCL as a basis: a title within a vertical market (if appropriate) that is interested in discussing or achieving one or more goals.

Creation of Sales Ready Messaging allows sales and marketing to collaborate, with the ultimate objective being to provide a superior buying experience. With this approach, some roles within organizations can be redefined in more tactical terms:

- *Tactical marketing.* This group owns and maintains Sales Ready Messaging with input from sales. Through all collateral and programs, it attempts to create curiosity and interest for each offering from among titles that are on the TCL. Curious buyers should be nurtured until they are ready to begin buying cycles. Attempts should be made to take titles on the TCL from a latent to an active need for offerings (migrate them from not looking to change to looking to do so).

- *Salespeople.* Once a goal is shared, they execute Sales Ready Messaging to develop buyer needs into a solution made up of a subset of usage scenarios from questioning templates developed jointly by sales and marketing.

Sales Ready Messaging becomes the heart of the marketing and sales engine to improve the buying experience. This messaging can be viewed as the integration of product and sales training, and it facilitates conversations with high-level buyers.

A few words about messaging:

- It is a journey rather than a destination, and it should be refined on a regular basis as marketing conditions and offerings change. Marketing is the control point, however, and salespeople should only execute the messaging provided if the process is going to be possible. If sales feels that the prompters need to be changed, constructive suggestions should be made, evaluated, and incorporated if appropriate.

- The higher within an organization a salesperson calls, the more predictable the conversations about business issues will be. There are levels within organizations below which structuring conversations will not be possible. Buyers that do not have enterprise business issues (users, lower-level managers, and so on) will be more focused on the product. Three things are necessary to structure sales calls in this manner: vertical segment, buyer title, and buyer goal.

- While we have discussed only prompters to be used during sales calls for offerings, there are several other aspects of messaging, such as prospecting letters and scripts, templates for selling professional services, call introductions, success stories, and so on.

Summary

Venture capitalists invest huge sums in companies, which in turn spend their capital to create new offerings, provide sellers with detailed product training, and expect them to go and make calls on all vertical markets and titles. This is a major challenge if CSM, marketing communications, and sales haven't provided a framework for doing so. We view the creation of Sales Ready Messaging as being part of the customer solution management costs. While we appreciate that some industry knowledge and training is necessary, some of the product training budget could be reallocated to the creation of messaging.

By creating a TCL, an organization can steer salespeople toward the vertical segments and titles that it wants them to call on. By having salespeople ask questions and empowering buyers, the organization can make the buying experience a sustainable competitive advantage by leveraging best practices within sales organizations while affording buyers control over the conversation.

We'll also show how this messaging allows organizations to help sellers align with the new buyers

MANAGING SALES TO FACILITATE THE BUYING PROCESS

C hoosing a VP of sales is an important decision. This is particularly important for fledgling companies with aggressive growth targets. CEOs making this decision generally fall into one of two categories:

- Those that have risen through the sales ranks and may themselves have been sales executives. Such people understand the challenges of the position and may be relieved to delegate the responsibility for generating top-line revenue. For some of these CEOs, a major benefit of running a company is that they no longer have to create (and defend) sales forecasts!

- Those who have no direct experience in selling or managing a sales organization. They usually view sales through the lens of the pervasive negative stereotype. Hiring to fill a position that they have little understanding of is a difficult decision, with a great deal riding on making the correct choice.

For organizations, managing expenses is relatively straightforward. The biggest issue in delivering expected profits is achieving top-line revenues, and that responsibility falls squarely on the shoulders of the VP of sales.

In our experience, CEOs with or without direct experience give their VP of sales free rein in running the sales organization. It is a rare CEO or VP of sales who views and defines selling as anything other than the traditional convincing, persuading, and so on. Blindly accepting this view has long-term implications and causes the sales executive to be seen as a deal maker who must deliver numbers so that the CEO can provide earnings guidance to investors. Neither the CEO nor the VP of sales is expending any mental energy on how to provide a better buying experience.

Companies strive to foster a culture that makes working for them a competitive advantage when recruiting. IBM, for example, has always considered showing respect for the individual employee a cornerstone of its success. Google has created an atmosphere that provides flexibility in people's work schedules, many perks to make

the office an environment that people enjoy, and freedom in how people do their jobs that encourages (and demands) creativity.
Companies that are successful in creating this work environment
enjoy huge advantages in recruiting and retaining the best people in
the workforce.

Companies that take extraordinary care of their employees enjoy
the significant benefit of having reduced turnover. Yet turnover within
the sales organization often mirrors that of companies that don't create a great culture for employees. Salespeople are a different breed.
Companies don't know how to pamper them. Most sellers are in satel-
lite or branch offices, so they have minimal exposure to the
headquarters location. The nature of their relationship with a company is more financial: the compensation plan, car allowance, expense
policy, and so on. The most common reason that salespeople leave or
are told to leave is that they aren't making their numbers.

There are three reasons that people or organizations don't change
their behavior:

Will not. They have a motivation or attitude issue.

Cannot. There is a skill or knowledge issue: they don't know *how* to
    change.

Oblivious. They are unaware that there is a problem or that a higher
    level of sales performance is expected.

Despite compelling reasons to change, the pervasive attitude is
that sales has always been the way it is and that nothing is going to
change it. Given the way buyers are changing how they buy, this
assumption is more dangerous than ever for the long term. Even
among companies that want to change the sales environment, most
don't know how. Compounding matters, the landscape is rife with
"burn victims" that have tried to implement sales training, CRM, or a
sales process, but have failed. If it were easy, more companies would
be doing it.

In our estimation, there is a direct negative implication of failing to better support sales. Even companies that have created positive cultures for nonsales employees fail to show the same concern and respect for buyers. They pay lip service, using phrases like "The customer is number one" or "The customer is always right," among others, but they have no mechanism for treating buyers in a way that differentiates them from the competition while buying decisions are being made. Customer care and support can positively benefit customers, but what about prospects?

It is ironic that these same companies invest huge sums in product development, hoping that their offering can provide a sustainable competitive advantage. Yet product cycles ebb and flow as competitors make announcements. The holy grail of a sustainable competitive advantage can be the way an organization sells, but this requires that fundamental changes be made throughout the company to achieve that objective, fueled by leadership from senior executives.

What Are You Managing?

Failure to devise a better sales environment eliminates the possibility of defining and delivering positive buying experiences with any consistency. During a sales cycle, a prospect's primary contact is the salesperson. His buying experience (whether he buys or not) shapes his opinions of vendors. As we've mentioned earlier in the book, this perception becomes more important every day as social networking continues to emerge as a way to gather transparent information about vendors, their offerings, their support, and so on. The salesperson shapes what the prospect perceives, and the prospect has the means to share this positive or negative perception easily with literally millions of others.

In shaping the B2B buying experience, the salesperson most strongly influences the outcome. Sellers that provide better buying experiences will often prevail, even though they don't have better pricing or superior offerings. First-level sales managers have the responsibility for assessing and developing people, but how do you manage eight people when you don't know how they are positioning your offerings (what conversations they are having with buyers) during sales calls? Just as no two snowflakes are identical, sales calls made by different members of a sales team can have little in common.

It should also be noted that the actions of first-level sales managers are more involved with monitoring "selling skills" than with measuring the ability to facilitate buying. You can see the mountain that a sales manager must climb if she is going to develop people to provide better buying experiences. Most managers have their hands full just staying focused on delivering top-line revenue targets. Without a process, it is difficult for them to assess and develop their direct reports.

Fumbling the Handoff

Companies that fail to get product marketing aligned with their selling efforts face major organizational obstacles that by default get passed on to first-level managers and salespeople. A new hire goes through orientation and product training before being assigned a quota and a territory. New hires join with diverse backgrounds, having worked for different companies, been exposed to different types of sales training, had different experience, and exhibited varying degrees of competence in the facets of the sales cycle.

Once they are assigned quotas, salespeople are given a great deal of latitude in how they sell. This is a euphemistic way of saying that few sales organizations have an executable standard approach to selling. According to CSO Insights, only 32 percent of sales executives claim to have a formal sales process. If these organizations were audited on how thoroughly their processes were implemented and/or how closely they reflected how people buy, that number would shrink considerably. Compare that to back office functions such as accounting, where companies must have a formal process. Without sales, accounting would not be required for very long, so why do we accept the lack of a repeatable, auditable process in the selling environment?

When you step back and consider it, positioning offerings in most sales organizations nets out to the words and phrases that come from each salesperson's lips. What percentage of sellers is up to this formidable task?

These and other factors make sales both a lucrative career and a "sink or swim" proposition. It should come as no surprise that a high percentage of the people that are hired never produce revenue at the expected levels. New hires (and all salespeople, for that matter) have no choice but to make several important decisions on their own:

- What vertical markets are they to pursue? This decision is potentially influenced by their experience and background.

- What titles do they target and call on within each vertical market?

- How do they generate initial interest?

- Once a buyer expresses interest, how to do they position the firm's offerings, either by trying to tell (sell) buyers or by formulating questions to ask (empower buyers)?

- What constitutes a qualified opportunity?

Managing Activity

After a 90-day honeymoon period, the new hire is under pressure to show *activity*. This creates the expectation that he will have a list of "qualified" opportunities in his pipeline. As you can imagine, inept or desperate sellers will be concerned about quality only if and when they have sufficient quantity. Sales managers, of course, want to believe because firing a sales rep means replacing him and starting the process over again. What percentage of new salespeople remains in your company two years after being hired?

Some companies have defined pipeline milestones that at least provide a road map for progressing through the sales cycle. The question is, how many of those milestones are measurable or auditable events, as opposed to salespeople's opinions on where they are in the process? Some sellers will purposely be overly optimistic, while others may believe that they are further along than they actually are. Either has an adverse effect on the quality of the opportunities in the pipeline.

In the environment that we just described, the sales manager's job stretches far beyond the abilities of mere mortals. Without a standard approach, ramp-up times are extended, and that quickly translates into quota pressure as sellers fall behind their year-to-date targets. Managers have a finite amount of time that can be allocated to each salesperson (for making joint calls, coaching, and so on). Ultimately, sales managers without a process morph into administrators monitoring activity within pipelines without an accurate way to measure progress. The focus is on the quantity of effort, and they have minimal ability to exert their influence to have a positive impact on the quality of effort. Some would say that managers ask sellers to work harder, but are unable to get them to work smarter.

Mandating the number of sales calls per day, prospecting calls per week, demos per month, and proposals or quotes per month can give the illusion of control, but it won't yield the desired result for many salespeople. We'll be kind and merely say that this pressure to meet objectives is unlikely to have a positive effect on the buying experience.

Without having "rules of the road" for consistent positioning of offerings to different vertical markets and titles, how can

- Marketing support selling efforts?

- Managers qualify or disqualify "opportunities"?

- Managers develop salespeople?

- Companies provide a consistent buying experience?

- Companies predict revenue from the pipeline?

The answer is: not very well. It should come as no surprise that *only 44 percent of salespeople achieve or exceed their quota each year.* Companies focus on productivity, quality, and other such measures in many areas of their business, but sales has been an area that has been difficult to improve.

Messaging as a Foundation

In stark contrast, consider the experience of new hires that join a company that has effectively executed customer solution management. During product training, they are given a road map for how to manage their territory and make their numbers. For each defined vertical market, they are shown

- A list of titles of people who are likely to be involved in selling, funding, and implementing each offering

- For each title they are given, a list of high-probability business issues that can be addressed through the use of a specific offering

- For each vertical market, title, and goal combination they are given, a template that positions only those features or capabilities that are relevant to achieving the goal, along with diagnostic questions to ask to uncover which features the buyer feels are relevant

This Sales Ready Messaging facilitates the sharing of best practices, makes the positioning of offerings more consistent, and begins to make the buyer experience more predictable.

This is a function of empowering buyers to buy at two different levels:

1. The templates contain nothing but questions, so the buyer has a great degree of control over the call. Asking relevant, intelligent

questions that buyers are capable of answering goes a long way toward creating a better buying experience.

2. The templates are indexed by buyer goals, so the buying cycle begins when and if a buyer shares a business goal that she wants to achieve. After diagnosing the reasons that the buyer can't achieve better results with her current method, the seller knows with a high degree of certainty which capabilities the buyer is likely to need. To be sure, these capabilities are presented in yes/no questions. The final step is to ask the buyer whether, if she had the capabilities to which she responded yes, she could achieve her desired goal.

Calls made in this way are consistent and respectful of buyers. Manipulation is eliminated because the buyer's answers dictate her "solution." Even though the sales manager wasn't on the call, the outcome has been defined, as that solution must be some or all of the capabilities that were mapped to the buyer goal.

Having Sales Ready Messaging created for all major offerings takes a tremendous burden off the shoulders of salespeople and allows companies to create functional descriptions of a manager's job. By "loading the lips" of the salesperson for making calls on key players, the benefit goes far beyond creating questioning templates. If a manager knows that buying cycles begin when a goal is shared or a problem (the inverse of a goal) is admitted, and knows that sellers have questioning templates that position capabilities relative to goals, the potential outcomes of sales calls has been defined:

- The buyer's solution has to be some subset of the capabilities that were mapped to helping the buyer achieve his goal (the right side of the prompter).

- After a goal has been shared, the seller started by asking questions to uncover which capabilities the buyer is likely to need (the left side of the prompter).

Aligning with Expert Buyers

Sales calls can involve either expert or nonexpert buyers. Some common characteristics of calls with nonexperts are

1. They are proactive contacts by salespeople with titles from the TCL.

2. The calls are heavily focused on business issues rather than offerings.

3. Buyers are "blank canvases," meaning that they have few, if any, preconceived notions or requirements.

4. No other vendors are involved.

In such cases, the buyer is in Phase 1 of the buying curves model, and after a goal is shared, a diagnosis using Sales Ready Messaging should be in alignment with the conversation that the buyer wants to have.

Calls with expert or knowledgeable buyers have different characteristics:

1. Often they are inbound calls from people at lower levels within an organization.

2. The discussions are much more feature/offering focused.

3. The buyers have opinions on what they believe their requirements are.

4. The buyers may have spoken with other vendors already.

As you can imagine, initiating buying cycles at high levels will yield a high win rate, but there are many instances in which knowledgeable buyers contact sellers. Trying immediately to have a buyer share a goal and do a diagnosis will not align with a buyer who has already established her requirements. As soon as a seller either challenges these requirements or tries to add new ones to the list, the buyer will feel that she is being manipulated, and her buying experience heads in the wrong direction. For these reasons, we suggest that these buyers should be handled differently.

An approach that we refer to as interest qualification (IQ) should be used with buyers who have already determined their requirements. Let's assume that such a buyer calls a seller and show you the suggested steps as follows:

- Establish credibility.

- Learn the buyer's requirements.

- Try to discover what the business drivers behind the evaluation are.

- For each business driver, ask what specific requirements will be needed.

- Start a diagnosis to try to uncover additional requirements by asking questions.

We'd like to provide an example of a dialogue that would take place between a sales operations manager who has done research on CRM and is now calling a salesperson to learn more about her offering:

Buyer: "This is Rob Sherman of the Acme Company. I'm interested in learning more about your CRM software."

Seller: "I'd be happy to help you. What prompted you to contact us?"

Buyer: "I spent some time looking at your Web site."

Seller: "What type of company is Acme?"

Buyer: "We offer consulting services to the banking industry."

Seller: "What is your area of responsibility within Acme?"

Buyer: "I'm the sales operations manager."

Seller: "Based upon your research so far, what, if any, requirements have you established for CRM?"

Buyer: "We'd like hosted software, we want the ability to customize milestones, and we want to do business with a vendor that has experience with professional services companies."

Seller: "That's helpful for me to know. I'm wondering what business drivers are behind your organization's evaluation of CRM offerings."

At this point, the buyer may share a goal that is on the TCL that the vendor has provided to the seller. If so, the seller would ask what specific capabilities the buyer felt were needed to achieve that goal. It is possible that the buyer hasn't mapped capabilities to goals, so this would be a worthwhile discussion to have. The seller would then begin to execute the left side of the Solution Development Prompter for the appropriate goal.

If the buyer did not share a goal, it is likely that she is unaware of the business drivers or is not yet convinced that the seller is competent. In either event, we suggest asking questions that get the buyer talking about potential areas of difficulty that are included in the TCL. If and when the buyer shares a goal, the seller can then begin to execute the Solution Development Prompter. A seller's worst case is that no goal is shared, as we'll now show you:

Seller: "What type of system are you using today, and how do sales managers review pipelines?"

Buyer: "There is no formal system. Most sales managers have salespeople provide Excel spreadsheets so that they can review opportunities."

Seller: "How often are the spreadsheets updated?"

Buyer: "It depends on the salesperson, but often only toward the end of a month, when forecasts are due."

Seller: "How do sellers learn about previous activities in newly assigned accounts?"

Buyer: "Because we have no centralized system today, that is largely dependent on the records that the previous seller kept. As you can imagine, the information is likely to be more complete if the previous seller is still with our company. When a seller leaves or is terminated, the detail is far more sketchy."

Seller: "Has that caused you to miss potential opportunities or to have new sellers ask buyers to update them?"

Buyer: "While the system isn't ideal, I don't think this has been a major issue for us."

Seller: "How do managers track opportunities as they proceed through the pipeline?"

Buyer: "That largely depends on the sales manager. Most of them will track major opportunities by talking with the salesperson. Worst case, on a monthly basis, the managers review the updates in the forecast."

At this point, the seller is about five minutes into the call. No goal has been shared, so no buying cycle has begun. Before he runs out of time, we suggest that the seller offer a menu of potential goals from the TCL.

Seller: "Rob, I appreciate your describing your current environment, and that has been helpful to me. In working with other professional services companies, we find that their objectives for CRM include

1. Improving forecast accuracy

2. Driving higher revenues

3. Shortening start-up times for new hires

4. Increasing cross-selling revenue

Do any of these align with your objectives for CRM?"

At this point, the hope is that the buyer will choose one or more of the goals offered. If he chooses more than one, the seller can ask which one should be discussed first. Before beginning with the questions on the left side of the prompter, the seller should ask what capabilities the buyer feels could help Acme achieve the goal. This enables the seller to understand the requirements that the buyer has already established.

If the buyer does not share a goal, the seller can ask who within Acme could provide the business drivers and see if she can gain access to that person. If the buyer is unwilling to provide access, the seller can offer to e-mail success stories for clients in the professional services space and follow up at a later time.

The net result is that if a buyer will not or cannot share a business goal (what potential value can be realized), a buying cycle has not begun, and it is unlikely that continuing will result in a favorable buying decision. Rather than allow each seller to handle an inbound call, sales organizations can map out a best practices approach to having buyers share business goals.

Managing Pipeline with a Process

Once salespeople have learned to execute messaging, organizations have the luxury of having the manager serve as a second set of eyes in allowing opportunities to enter the pipeline. This is critical when you consider the cost of wasting resources on unqualified accounts.

After executing a prompter, the salesperson should be able to answer the following debriefing questions:

- *The company, the buyer's title, and the goal(s) shared.* The goal would come from the TCL menu for that title.

- *Reasons that the buyer can't achieve the goal in her current environment.* This information is learned by asking the diagnostic questions contained in the template.

- *Capabilities needed.* This includes all of the usage scenarios that the buyer agreed were needed to achieve the goal being discussed.

- *Value.* If possible, the seller should quantify the potential improvement that could be realized if the buyer had the capabilities discussed.

   A step that is taken after the call would be to determine which other titles would be likely to be involved in selling, funding, and implementing the offering in question.

   If a salesperson can answer those debriefing question, then he has made an effective call, and the opportunity looks promising. Our suggestion is that he write an e-mail or a snail mail letter to the buyer that contains all of this information, and in that letters to request access to the other titles that the seller would like to call on, as shown in Figure 10-1.

   Documenting the call in this manner accomplishes many things:

1. It refreshes the buyer's recollection of the issues that were discussed and establishes that the salesperson listened.

2. It distinguishes the salesperson from competitors who either don't document calls or provide letters with minimal content other than thanking buyers for their time.

3. The capabilities listed can serve as a script for internal selling to help the buyer explain what she is interested in buying. Instead of leading with product, the buyer can recount the business goals, the reasons they can't be accomplished now, and the capabilities that need to be improved.

4. After documenting the call, the buyer requests access to other titles, as well as the ability to meet or talk with the buying committee after calling on everyone to reach consensus on whether or not to proceed with an evaluation of the offering.

5. The letter becomes an auditable document for the sales manager, and if the buyer agrees to give access to the titles requested, this

is a measurable action that a manager can grade as having achieved a pipeline milestone (our recommendation is that a buyer who agrees with the content of the letter and grants access to others becomes a Champion).

Requiring such a letter allows first-level managers to perform quality control checks to ensure that only qualified opportunities are graded as being at a "C" (Champion) level. Gaining access to other titles can be audited as well, as those calls should be documented in the same manner (without the request for access). This enables a sales

---

Dear Steve,

Thank you for your interest in ABC Systems. The purpose of this letter is to summarize my understanding of our discussion and determine the next steps moving forward.

Qualification Elements:
1. Goal(s)
2. Current situation
3. Capabilities
4. Value
5. Access to key players

Primary Business Goals
You told me that your primary goal is achieving profit targets by forecasting more accurately.

Summary of Current Situation
Today, reps update opportunity status on a monthly basis, managers have trouble identifying stalled opportunities so that they can make suggestions, close rates vary widely by salesperson, and you sometimes have trouble getting the latest status on "make or break" opportunities.

Capabilities Required/Potential Benefit
You feel you could improve forecasting accuracy by 25 percent if you had the following capabilities:
• After making calls, salespeople would be prompted on their laptops to report progress against a standard set of company milestones for each opportunity in their pipeline.

manager to monitor not only activity but, more important, progress. A higher-quality pipeline will minimize high-pressure quarter ends.

Once a seller has spoken with all of the requested titles (using the Sales Ready Messaging prompters), a conference call or meeting can be scheduled to decide whether or not to proceed with the evaluation. If agreement is reached, our recommendation is that the seller negotiate a sequence of events (SOE) that lists the steps needed to make a recommendation that is consistent with how the prospect wants to buy and to include estimated dates for each step that the buyers agree to.

- When reviewing a salesperson's pipeline, sales managers could access the pipeline database, evaluate the status of specific opportunities, and e-mail suggestions to reps to improve their chances of winning the business.
- On an ongoing basis, the system could track historical close rates for each salesperson by milestone, and apply them to each of the salesperson's opportunities to allow you to predict revenue.
- When trying to determine the status of large opportunities, you or any C-level executive could access your pipeline anytime/anywhere, and review progress against milestones without needing to talk to anyone in your sales organization.

You expressed interest in further investigating ABC Systems. I'd like to propose the following next steps:

1. Confirm that you are in agreement with the summary of our discussion.
2. Arrange interviews with your CFO and CIO, who would be involved in the implementation of a CRM system.
3. Summarize findings to the group and gain consensus for further evaluation of our offerings.

I'll call Tuesday, January 7, at 9 a.m. to review this letter and discuss our next steps. I look forward to working with you.

Best,
Rob Acker

Figure 10-1 *Champion Letter*

Part of empowering people to buy is to align with their buying process in terms of steps, but agreeing to the pace of the evaluation minimizes the chance that buyers will feel rushed or pressured. Once agreement to continue with evaluating an offering is reached, we suggest the following steps:

- The seller asks the committee to describe its buying process. If a vague answer is provided, sellers should ask questions to draw the members out, such as

  When would purchasing be involved?

  What is the turnaround on contracts with legal?

  Is it necessary to get on a preferred vendor list, and what does that entail?

  What is the time frame for making a buying decision?

- The seller can then present an SOE that contains the steps that the vendor needs to take in order to make a formal written recommendation. These steps should be reviewed and explained as necessary.

- The seller can end the meeting by agreeing to combine steps in the buying process with steps from his SOE, with the intent of providing a draft copy of how the evaluation will proceed. This draft, complete with estimated dates, would then be agreed to and would become the road map for moving forward. We suggest that there should be some go/no-go steps that would allow either party to withdraw. Without this flexibility, the buying committee may feel that it is being asked for a firm commitment of several weeks by a pushy salesperson.

  Figure 10-2 shows a sample SOE.

We don't want salespeople to use a sledgehammer when a tack hammer will do the job, so SOEs are used on fairly large opportunities, and the number of steps will vary depending on the size and complexity of the offering. On small transactions at decision-maker

Week of	Checkpoint	Activities	Billable	Responsibility
May 28	✓	Prove capabilities to committee members		CRM Inc.
June 9		Survey current system	$20K	CRM Inc.
June 11	✓	Implementation plan developed with IT		Both
June 11		Share survey results and provide estimated cost		CRM Inc.
June 18	✓	Facilitate cost versus benefit analysis		Both
June 18		Define success metrics		Both
June 18		Complete vendor application form		CRM Inc.
July 4	✓	Add CRM Inc. to approved vendor list		Acme
July 11		Corporate visit		Both
July 18	✓	Conduct predecision review		CRM Inc.
July 25	✓	Deliver proposal		CRM Inc.
Aug 2		Begin implementation		Both

*At each checkpoint, our companies will mutually decide whether or not to proceed.

Figure 10-2 *Acme Sequence of Events*

levels, we've seen instances where the SOE and the champion letter are merged into a single document.

Once an SOE has been agreed to, the manager can review it and at that point grade the prospect an "E" (Evaluation). The manager can also monitor progress based on the steps that have been completed. If steps are slipping, that may be an indication that something has gone awry, and the manager may want to have a conversation or make a call with the salesperson. SOEs will typically be updated and republished about once a month.

The SOE provides a vehicle that allows the buyer to exert some control over how and when an offering will be evaluated. It also serves as a road map for both parties as to when resources are going to be needed. Buyers also like to have some idea of where they are in the buying process. A few major benefits accrue to vendors that put SOEs in place:

- They align with buyers and can provide a better buying experience.

- They have a high degree of commitment if a committee will agree to an SOE.

- They have an estimated close date that the buying committee has agreed to. This can have a significantly positive effect on forecasting accuracy in that sellers tend to be overoptimistic. If a seller forecasts that an opportunity will close in April and May, but it ultimately closes in June, her forecasting accuracy is only 33.3 percent even though she won the business!

- Having SOEs in place give the sales management team visibility to identify potential revenue shortfalls early enough to take steps to mitigate the situation.

- SOEs make it more difficult to close before buyers are ready to buy.

With a sales process, Sales Ready Messaging, and the ability to audit opportunities and measurable milestones, the roles of salespeople and sales managers can be redefined.

A salesperson is responsible for executing Sales Ready Messaging and documenting calls in a way that enables her sales manager to grade her pipeline.

Sales managers project a sales cycle ahead to ensure that pipelines are sufficient to achieve quota. They grade pipelines starting from Champion by auditing documentation. By identifying blockages in each seller's pipeline, they identify skill deficiencies and work to shore them up.

Summary

A sales process must be supported top-down within an organization. One of the fundamental decisions is how sales is going to be defined, as that goes a long way toward how buyers are going to be viewed and treated. Getting customer solution marketing, marketing communications, and sales on the same page is a prerequisite for being able to provide a superior buying experience on a consistent basis. To do so, Sales Ready Messaging should reflect best practices, and sellers should mostly be asking rather than telling in sales calls.

By executing messaging, sellers should be able to document calls in a way that allows managers to grade their pipelines objectively based on tangible events rather than on sellers' subjective opinions. Sellers are under pressure to build a pipeline, but they often emphasize quantity rather than quality. Qualifying a Champion, getting access to titles on the TCL, and, when possible, negotiating SOEs allow salespeople to win rather than merely keep busy.

Ultimately, the buying cycle should be a merger of how buyers want to buy and what steps vendors have to take in order to produce a recommendation (proposal) that reflects what buyers need. The big question for vendors is: Am I treating buyers the way I'd like to be treated when making a buying decision? Being able to honestly answer yes can be a competitive advantage that transcends price and product advantages.

MAGIC MOMENTS: CREATING A GREAT CUSTOMER EXPERIENCE

*The reason I'm so obsessed with these drivers of the customer experi-
ence is that I believe that the success we have had over the past 12 years
has been driven exclusively by that customer experience. We are not
great advertisers. So we start with customers, figure out what they want,
and figure out how to get it to them.*

—Jeff Bezos, CEO, Amazon.com

S tart with customers, figure out what they want, and figure out
how to get it to them. Is there a simpler, yet more powerful concept in all of business?

This quote by Jeff Bezos appeared in the *New York Times* in January 2008. The article, titled "Put Buyers First? What a Concept,"
shared the story of the author's experience with the purchase of a
PlayStation 3, a $500 item, as a Christmas present for one of his sons.
The item never arrived, or at least the author didn't receive it. When
he logged on to track his package, something that Amazon makes it
very easy to do, he was distraught to learn that the package not only
had been shipped, but in fact had been delivered to his apartment
building. None of his neighbors reported having seen it, and gloom set
in as he realized that it had been stolen. This was, of course, not Amazon's fault. Still, he called the Amazon customer service representative
to explain the situation. Astonishingly, Amazon sent a replacement
once it verified the original one had been purchased and shipped. It
was delivered on Christmas Eve.

As we said earlier in this book, customers talk about their experiences with vendors, typically sharing more negative experiences than
positive ones. Perhaps an exception exists when customers receive
truly outstanding customer *care*. The word *care* has been emphasized,
because is there a better example of truly caring for your customer
than what Amazon demonstrated in this example? And what a memorable experience! Here was an experience that the customer was
obviously willing—indeed, eager—to share with the world.

We'll come back to this Amazon example later. For now, let's contrast this great example of customer care with two real-life examples that the authors of this book experienced in 2008. One was with Sears, and one was with Apple.

The Sears Saga—by Tim Young

For most people, the idea of building a new home is an exciting concept, providing them with the opportunity to create the world that they want, their perfect place. After the home layout is determined, a daunting list of decisions must be confronted. Should we install carpet or wood floors, or both? What color and style? And then there are the light fixtures, paint colors, tile, and other accents to be decided. This decision dance usually involves a series of entertaining discussions between husband and wife if this is a family move, as it was in my case.

Building our new home gave us the opportunity to choose appliances that fit into our image of a dream kitchen design. Finally, we could have double ovens, gas cooktops, a dishwasher with noise and disturbance levels that weren't measured on the Richter scale, and a roomy refrigerator with convenience features. Naturally we wanted long-lasting, stylish, and functional appliances, but we also wanted value.

A quick Internet search for premium kitchen appliances returned a number of brands, such as Viking and Wolf, as well as several forums where real users discussed the pros and cons of each. After a quick review of the forums, we opted to give Sears a try. Yes, that Sears, the one that began as the R. W. Sears Watch Company in Minneapolis in 1886, before moving to Chicago the following year. One hundred twenty-three years later, the firm had moved beyond being the mail-order answer to farmers' prayers, offering a high-end appliance line dubbed Kenmore Pro. Given that we live in a rural setting, we were reassured because Sears had physical locations within a reasonable drive, where we could see the appliances and, we assumed, get support if there were ever problems. The Kenmore Pro line looked sleek as well, with brushed platinum, so we opted for the double oven, gas cooktop, refrigerator, and dishwasher. The dimensions were given to the builder, and nothing was left but to wait the eight months until the construction was far enough along so that the appliances could be installed.

If you've ever built a house, you know how exciting it is to have the seemingly never-ending final weeks *finally* come to an end. At last, move-in day was upon us. After unpacking and getting settled in, we realized that we were hungry. And so we turned the dial on the top of our double oven to preheat and carried some boxes upstairs. By the time we reached the top of the stairs, we smelled something burning. We rushed downstairs to the oven and saw that the temperature was off the chart at over 550 degrees. The oven was locked and had, for some reason, thrown itself into self-clean mode. We shut it off, wondered what had happened, and tried again. The oven would respond only with a bizarre error code that was nowhere in the manual. We called Sears and informed it of the situation. The customer service representative said that he would schedule a technician to come out and look. In a week! Our pleading was to no avail; this was, he assured us, the soonest the technician could get there.

We spent the next six days enjoying our new home and cursing Sears. Finally, the technician, who was actually a local contractor and not a Sears employee, rang the doorbell. He diagnosed the problem, thought he had fixed it, and turned on the oven, only to repeat the experience we had had. He then got on the phone to Sears (wasn't *he* Sears?), and, after a lengthy call, hung up and told us that the oven had a bad sensor that would have to be replaced. "How long?" we asked. "Four or five days" was his reply.

And so it was that, two weeks after we had moved in, the same technician came back with the sensor, only to find that, when it had been installed, the problem continued. Another phone call with Sears ensued, this time resulting in our being told that the oven was defective and would have to be replaced. By this point we were not really surprised and had gone completely negative on Sears. But things were going to get worse.

A week later, the oven arrived via truck and was placed in our garage, but no one had been scheduled to install it. Of course, the delivery guys in the Sears truck knew nothing about this. We called and arranged a time for a morning installation, but no one showed up. When we called to find out why, we were told that the oven couldn't be installed until we had someone uninstall the defective oven! Amazingly, this issue had escaped the customer service people when they agreed to schedule the installation.

I will spare you the countless heated calls and e-mails we had with the Sears "customer care" people. We pleaded our case and explained the situation, all to no avail. I'll further spare you the recounting of a problem with the refrigerator after two weeks: it stopped working, forcing us to find a home for everything in the refrigerator and freezer until it could be fixed a week later (by someone local that *we paid* to fix it, since Sears had said that it would take three weeks). Rather, let's just say that we paid to have the oven uninstalled so that Sears could come out and install the new oven, which finally worked—five weeks after we moved in.

The chain of e-mails and phone calls to Sears's customer care group would have made a perfect script for a training video on how *not* to treat customers. I always escalated the call, and more than once I had a Sears supervisor hang up on me. I was promised callbacks that never happened.

Many years ago, very early in my business career, I learned this simple formula for customer satisfaction:

Perception – expectations = satisfaction

As the buyer, what were my expectations?

1. The appliances would work as advertised.

2. If there should be a problem, Sears would stand behind its 123-year-old brand and make it right.

Clearly, based on this experience, I was beyond dissatisfied. In fact, I was irate. As we indicated that unhappy buyers are likely to do, I told the world via blog posts, forum comments, and, in general, honest (negative) assessments of my experience to anyone within earshot.

Sears may have earned the status of a highly recognizable brand during its long history, but in this instance it did nothing to earn a reputation for caring about its customer. So the appliance was broken. Did Sears have an opportunity to turn this from a negative into a positive experience, just as Amazon did? Sure. Instead, it made the situation much, much worse.

A Bad Apple—by John Holland

Choosing a company that has a great product and a great reputation is no guarantee of a positive buying experience. A few years ago, one of our daughters was starting law school and needed a new laptop. She had started with Macs at home as a child. While she was at college, she had bought a Windows machine and had experienced both hardware and virus issues, so she decided to buy a new Mac laptop. The order was placed with a two-week cushion before she was to start school, and we received notification that the machine would be delivered within three days.

When she called to check, she found out that her laptop had been mistakenly delivered to and accepted by a health-care facility, and her delivery would be delayed by a few days. That didn't present any problem. Three days later, we were informed that the health-care facility would not release the machine and that a new order could not be placed until the machine was returned. A week passed before we escalated the situation to the next level. We were told that there was not a single laptop available for delivery in the entire United States. Calls were made on a daily basis until we had escalated the situation to the highest level that we could.

The laptop was finally delivered two weeks after my daughter had started law school. A VP of customer care ultimately contacted her, was very apologetic about the delay, extended the warranty, and provided an Airport (wireless) unit at no charge. While this was an attempt to save face, there was no good way to make up for her having to start the first two weeks of school without her laptop. This goes to show that a great reputation and a great offering won't overcome customer service issues. This also comes from a longtime Mac user who had had several positive experiences in the past.

What Makes a MAGIC Moment?

At the start of this chapter, we shared the positive buying experience that the *New York Times* writer had with Amazon. Why was the customer so eager to tell the world about that experience? I think it's because most of us want to feel special, to feel cared for, and to experience that special treatment for ourselves. It's a form of pampering. Using the metaphor of a customer care bank account, I'd say that Amazon made a few deposits with the customer that day that will pay for any minor misgivings later—misgivings that, given my own personal experience with Amazon, are very unlikely to occur.

When you call customer service, how often do you get the feeling that the person speaking with you seems like the first line of defense, rather than an employee who is empowered to do the right thing to ensure your satisfaction? Surely you have experienced this for yourself. This makes the Amazon example all the more remarkable. How did it come to pass that the customer care representative at Amazon agreed to ship a new PlayStation 3 to the customer? Was there a supervisor listening in on the call who gave her the green light? Does Amazon have a policy of asking no questions and just giving the customer what he asks for? No, more likely, Amazon has accomplished something that is far more elusive for most organizations, more sustainable, and much, much more valuable. Evidently, it has successfully created a culture that makes customer satisfaction a priority and empowers employees to make the decisions that they believe are best for the customer first and for Amazon second. In fact, this was probably a good long-term decision for Amazon based upon future business that will come its way. Too often, vendors merely focus on the transaction at hand (as Sears and Apple did in the examples we shared).

A business culture can evolve either accidentally or deliberately with guidance, but make no mistake: it will evolve. Rarely do you see "culture" listed in business plans that are presented to investors as a strategic asset, weapon, or differentiating factor. This strikes us as odd, considering that there are few competitive advantages that are more sustainable and defensible than a pervasive culture, whether it is geared toward customer-focused innovation (think 3M traditionally and Google currently), customer-focused design and styling (think Toyota traditionally and Apple currently), or customer care (think FedEx traditionally and Amazon currently).

Unhappy Employees = Unhappy Customers

It is surprising to see the degree to which companies focus internally on products rather than on customers. We discussed this inside-out perspective in Chapter 9, "Getting Product Marketing Right." This is even more critical for service-oriented companies and, let's face it, aren't most businesses becoming service businesses in one way or another? A company may have a great product at a great price, but if the customer experience isn't at least up to par, customers will wander until they find a company where it is. Ask yourself: If I were to buy my company's product, what kind of experience would I expect? What kind of service would I expect if something went wrong?

You could make a strong argument that ensuring a great customer experience begins with ensuring a great employee experience. Employees who are engaged, inspired, motivated, appreciated, and empowered are generally happy—happy to work for the employer, happy to represent its products and services, happy to speak with customers, and happy to help make customers . . . well, happy.

Happiness begets happiness, and it all starts with focusing on the employees. And that means a top-down culture that's supported by the CEO, the board of directors, and the senior management team. If you question whether it needs to be top-down and employee focused, let's look at yet one more example.

A Good Apple

Few companies have undergone the transformation that Apple Computer has in the past decade. After suffering through intense competition, market decline, and a record low stock price under the leadership of a string of CEOs, founder Steve Jobs took the helm permanently in 2000. Since that time, Apple has become an innovator and leader in personal music devices (iPod), cellular phones (iPhone) and, believe it or not, personal computers. The latter category is one in which Apple remains a small player, but it is also a category with tremendous upside, particularly now that Apple is effectively penetrating the corporate user market—and it's a category in which Apple has very enthusiastic and loyal supporters.

Apple has accomplished this by fostering a culture that's driven by customer-focused innovation and styling designed to support a broader multilegged product strategy. Its products command premium prices, and customers eagerly pay them. Despite the negative customer service experience reported earlier in this chapter, Apple customers overall are enthusiastic and loyal. For example, both authors of this book enthusiastically use Macs. So how did Apple go about putting employees first, as we suggested that companies should do if they're serious about having happy customers? As it turns out, it crafted a genius strategy.

The strategy behind the Apple Genius Bar may prove to be brilliant in more ways than one. You're familiar with the concept of software as a service (SaaS). The Genius Bar introduces the concept of hardware as a service (HaaS). Indeed, while almost all hardware-related tech support problems must be dealt with on the phone through a series of multinational and multiaccent transfers, Apple allows customers to get help in person. If your MacBook becomes ill or dies, you can schedule an appointment online (http://www.apple.com/retail/geniusbar) at your nearest Apple retail store Genius Bar. This type of convenience demonstrates a focus on what is easy for the *customer*, which, ironically, should also be convenient for Apple. Need an appointment on a Sunday? No problem; just schedule a visit in a store that is open on Sunday.

When you arrive, you'll see appointments clearly posted, and you'll be able to track the progress of your reservation. It's kind of like being at the deli, except that you can look at and play with all the cool toys in the store while you're waiting. When it's your turn, you'll get personal help from an Apple employee, who is dubbed a Genius and more often than not really will be. Your Mac (or iPod, iPhone, or Apple TV) will be fixed, or at least it will be diagnosed and your options will be clearly outlined for you. Many times problems are fixed right on the spot.

For many people, the entire customer experience is satisfying and boils down to three simple events: (1) the reservation, (2) the visit, and (3) the solution. In launching its HaaS strategy, Apple has clearly figured out that it's not just about the product, it's about the experience. Apple is right. That means not only user experience, but service experience as well.

But the genius strategy goes well beyond the employees in the stores, the ones who are dubbed Geniuses. What message is communicated to Apple employees by using the Genius moniker? Done properly, it becomes a self-fulfilling prophecy. All employees are expected to act in a certain way and to have the answers to the customer's problems. The moniker is supported by customer-friendly technology for making appointments and, we're sure, a leadership-driven culture that is focused on customers. The result is employees who feel empowered and appear to their customers to be geniuses. And that's a genius strategy!

B2B versus B2C

In the B2C examples we've shown, the salesperson's role is either non-existent or minimal. That speaks volumes about the state of selling. In B2B buying experiences, the seller plays a critical role. In the same way that a mediocre restaurant with a highly competent waiter can provide a better dining experience than a competitor with outstanding food but poor service, so it is with sellers.

It is one thing to win a B2B sale, often as a result of being perceived as being sincere and competent, but there is something else that is critical to the buying experience, and that is the expectations a seller sets concerning the usage of the offering that is being sold. Sellers that overstate or hype what their offering (or service and support) will deliver set the stage for a dissatisfied buyer. This is a price that vendors pay for leaving the positioning of offerings up to each individual salesperson.

With many B2B selling experiences, the salesperson is *the brand.* Imagine that your company has executed very well on product design, advertising, and PR. Your product is somewhat complex and expensive, so the sales cycle is several months. Before the buying cycle began, much of what the prospective buyer knew about your offering was from your Web site, PR, advertising, Webinars, videos, podcasts, blogs, and the like. Your company was able to create most of these communications in a vacuum and so had complete control.

After the prospective buyer expresses interest, he is handed off to a salesperson, who will be the face of the company for the remainder of the several-month buying process. During conversations with the prospective buyer, what will the salesperson say? How will she respond to certain questions? How will she represent your brand? Will you have any ability to control or influence what she says? Will it be at all consistent with the product and marketing messaging you've already deployed, or will the salesperson make it up on the fly?

Sure, there are tools such as Sales Ready Messaging by CustomerCentric Selling that are used enterprisewide to develop more consistent and customer-focused messaging. But most companies do not have a strategy for ensuring that the messaging is integrated and that the salesperson knows how to listen, how to respond, and what to say. Instead, most sales management is focused on ensuring that the salesperson (1) knows what his quota is and (2) has the skills needed to process and close sales. Notable by its absence is a focus by sales management on the quality of the customer experience.

In the end, the salesperson largely *is* the brand in the B2B customer experience. It's very telling that as we, and probably you, think of companies with great buying experiences, we think of B2C companies. Of course there are examples of small B2B companies that have enthusiastic supporters and deliver great buying experiences, but there are few on a larger scale.

Ironically, the ones that may fall into that category, such as Google (if you're an advertiser), have essentially eliminated the role of the salesperson. Imagine that you can log on, create an account, and easily spend $5,000, $10,000, or $50,000 or more a month on advertising without having to go through a salesperson to do it. Ten years ago, this would have required a (stereotypical) advertising salesperson that you might or might not have liked, along with lunches, dinners, and even golf outings.

In most B2B sales situations, however, the salesperson remains the essential part. We propose that companies make a top-down commitment to focusing on creating MAGIC moment experiences for their customers, and that means redefining the role of the salesperson and how her performance is measured.

Five Steps to Developing a MAGIC Moment Culture

1. *Measure what matters.* The old adage is that what gets measured is what gets done, so why not start with the end in mind? Develop a system for measuring the customer experience. This means ask-

ing your customers about their experience with you at every inter-action: Web, e-mail, phone, salesperson, billing, support, delivery, installation—you name it. And it may mean asking after every interaction, for a happy customer after a purchase may become a disgruntled customer six months later after a poor customer sup-port experience. Measure what matters and make the results highly visible for everyone.

2. *Articulate a vision focused on the customer.* This doesn't mean sending an e-mail to employees that says that customers are "job number one." Rather, it means articulating a vision in which you can achieve competitive uniqueness and advantage by how you ensure a great customer experience better than any competitive alternative can. Let investors, suppliers, and employees know that this is the key to your advantage, and that you will be measuring everything (see point 1) that affects the customer experience. When you ensure the best customer experience possible, your cus-tomers will advertise for you, you'll win repeat and referral business, and your employees will be engaged and enthusiastic about working for you. Everyone likes being on the winning team.

3. *Give your employees the power to become customer champions.* Let everyone, especially salespeople and customer-facing employees, know that you are measuring the customer experience (point 1) and that ensuring a great customer experience is central to your vision (point 2). Hold people and departments accountable for the quality of the customer experience, and eliminate bottlenecks that get in the way, such as departmental friction or "it's not my job" mentalities. If the customer experience isn't someone's job, then it is *everyone's* job.

4. *Interact with customers based on their preferences.* Provide many ways for customers to communicate with you based upon their preferences. This multichannel communication means e-mail, Web forms, chat, IM, telephone, mail, fax, or, in the case of Apple's genius strategy, in person. Make it easy for customers to

complain or to provide positive feedback, but be prepared to handle all inquiries properly and promptly. It is better for you not to offer a communication method (such as chat) if you cannot manage it properly than to offer it and provide a poor experience. Embrace every opportunity to communicate with customers.

5. *Compensate based on the customer experience.* In order to complete your cultural shift toward a MAGIC moment culture, you will need to tie your reward, recognition, and compensation systems to customer experience measurement. This can be individual, group, department, or companywide recognition.

The B2B Customer's Bill of Rights

Remember, in B2B sales, the salesperson is the brand. Therefore, we will close this chapter by sharing a list of what B2B buyers are coming to expect when they interact with salespeople. Customers are changing their behavior in ways that are dictating a different view of selling and a revised role for salespeople. Vendors can be eliminated from competition for not aligning with how buyers want to be treated. As you'll see as you review the list, traditional selling conflicts with many of these items.

The B2B Customer's Bill of Rights

1. "We don't want to feel manipulated."

2. "We don't want sellers trying to be our friends."

3. "We don't want to be pressured to buy."

4. "We don't want to feel that we have been sold. We want to be able to buy."

5. "We want to talk about our needs before being subjected to product pitches."

6. "We want sellers to help us get what *we* want."

7. "We don't want sellers stalking us."

8. "We don't want to be subjected to early or multiple trial closes."

9. "We want sellers to be honest about what their offerings can and can't do."

10. "We want our objections to be heard and considered before sellers try to talk us out of them."

11. "We don't mind sellers saying, 'I don't know, but I'll check and get back to you.'"

12. "We don't want sellers using terms that we don't fully understand."

13. "We want sellers to learn about our current procedures, then offer only the parts of their offerings that match the capabilities that we need in order to improve our business results."

14. "We want to be empowered to achieve our goals or solve our problems."

15. "We want sellers to have clear objectives and state them early in sales calls."

16. "We want sellers to provide facts about their companies rather than hype."

17. "We want sellers to be able to tell us in two sentences or less what it is that their companies do."

18. "We want to have sellers help us track actual results relative to expectations."

19. "We don't want to hear any more sellers' opinions on what they believe the value of their offering would be to us."

20. "We'd like cost versus benefits based upon our projections, not the seller's."

21. "We'd like sellers to understand and align with our buying processes."

22. "We don't want to have to wait until the end of the month to get a fair price."

23. "We don't want to hear sellers' opinions."

24. "We want to do business with sellers and companies that keep their commitments."

25. "We want sellers to respect the research we've done by treating us as being knowledgeable."

Summary

At a time when marketers often aspire to use technology tools to create viral marketing campaigns, the ultimate viral opportunities are staring us all in the face. Leaders of companies that foster environments that create great customer experiences have an opportunity to differentiate themselves from and outperform all their competitors. Recognizing, rewarding, and indeed engineering behavior that delivers MAGIC moments to customers would be an accomplishment that is difficult for competitors to match and difficult for customers to ignore. In a day and age of increasing commoditization and a ubiquitous focus on product features and benefits, leaders will emerge that use the way they sell as a sustainable competitive advantage. The question is, will you be one of those leaders?

12

USING A SALES PROCESS TO ACHIEVE A SUSTAINABLE COMPETITIVE ADVANTAGE

W hen you take anything beyond a cursory look, it is diffi-cult to deny that the buyer-seller relationship has been broken for some time and that vendors' actions are doing little to improve it. Many readers resent authors who describe prob-lems in graphic detail but do not offer an approach for resolving them. While our goal with this book has been to encourage readers to rethink the sales cycle and how they interact with buyers, we hope that the last few chapters have provided some tactical ways to achieve consistency in the positioning of offerings and improve the customer buying experience.

We've focused on higher-level challenges that organizations face when they try to improve the consistency and predictability of their sales efforts, thus achieving a sustainable competitive advantage by *how* they sell. There are a number of ways in which a vendor could approach establishing and implementing a process to gain control over the buying experience. In this case, let's look at how one methodol-ogy, CustomerCentric Selling, can be used toward that end.

In Chapter 3, we discussed how the awareness of a goal or prob-lem can surface. We gave an example of someone who needs a health scare before becoming motivated to reach and maintain a healthy weight. Status quo creeps into our lives and, predictably, lingers. Change presents challenges for individuals. Enterprise-level change can be exponentially more difficult because of the lack of individual ownership and the sheer number of people involved. However, when the requisite motivation is in place, enterprise change can take on a life of its own for the same reasons.

Recognition of either the rewards for successfully aligning with buyers or the negative consequences of failing to do so will fuel your efforts.

Vendors have done little over the last 50 years to treat buyers in a more honorable, respectful, and consistent manner. Accepting and reinforcing the traditional view of selling, providing standard product training, and turning over responsibility for the buying experience to each individual salesperson sow the seeds for sales mediocrity unless a vendor is enjoying a fleeting window in which it has the hottest product. During those periods, selling is made to look deceptively easy. Reality sets in when demand for the vendor's offerings cools or competitors raise the ante.

Buyers have been manipulated by sellers while making both B2C and B2B purchases. The bad experiences are the ones that they remember. As a result, buyers have a widespread mistrust of salespeople. Unfortunately, few vendors have seized the opportunity to change that dynamic. In giving up control of information by putting it on the Internet in the late 1990s, they put the keys needed for change into the hands of buyers. The challenge that vendors now face is aligning with the new buying behavior.

CEOs have allowed sales to languish in its current undesirable status quo. Imagine how dysfunctional a company would be if other departments had no defined relationships or rules for work flow. It wouldn't stay in business for long. In a manufacturing company, receiving has procedures for accepting raw materials into inventory. Inventory control provides raw materials to manufacturing, which passes finished goods into inventory. Order entry notifies inventory of what has to be shipped, and shipping notifies billing of what needs to be invoiced. There are fundamental "rules of the road" that are made at executive levels and must be followed by the members of each department.

Imagine being a CEO and walking a friend through your factory to show her these departments. During the tour, what would your friend see when you visited the sales department? If asked, how would you define the relationship between sales and marketing? While you would have multipage job descriptions for your VPs of sales and marketing, would there be any document giving a functional description of how those two departments interface?

We've all seen the poster "Nothing happens until somebody sells something," yet these two departments that share top-line revenue responsibility are largely left to their own devices. Blame and finger-pointing occur when the numbers aren't met, contributing to the perception of an "oil and water" relationship between marketing and sales. Without rules of the road, chaos reigns.

When we first published *CustomerCentric Selling* in 2003, we aimed to increase awareness that there could be a different approach to sales by using a process that captured and shared best practices. Most important, we espoused a philosophy of facilitating buying rather than selling to align with the fundamental human desire to exert control that buyers have when they are making buying decisions. We described in much greater detail than this book does our suggestions for using Sales Ready Messaging as the heart of a process that focused on buyer empowerment.

We've had many clients implement and realize significant benefits, but we wanted to share one story that we found remarkable.

In 2003, one of our clients shared an account situation that shows what is possible when buyers are treated with respect. A salesperson from our client was selling outsourced services to a division of a Fortune 500 company. It was a large transaction, and there were four other vendors competing for the business. The primary contact and ultimate decision maker was the director of procurement. At the end of the buying cycle, our client's salesperson was informed that he was being awarded the business and was asked to come to the account to finalize the transaction.

At the end of the meeting, the VP of procurement asked the seller how he had sold to them. George had never been asked that question before and wondered why she wanted to know. The VP explained that it had been the most professional and pleasant buying experience a vendor had ever provided. She had enjoyed agreeing to what steps had to be taken and the dates by which they should be completed. The seller indicated that he had used the CustomerCentric Selling methodology.

As surprising as that was, the VP of procurement attempted to have her VP of sales consider CCS because it could provide a competitive advantage. The VP of procurement proceeded to try to schedule an introductory call. While we wish we could tell you that this story had a happier ending, we don't want to lie. The VP of sales was "too busy" to talk with us. Having said that, this account shows that the manner in which an opportunity is sold (or buyers are allowed to buy) can and should provide a positive experience for the buyer and hopefully a competitive advantage. It also shows that many sales executives are highly skeptical that things can change for the better.

If *CustomerCentric Selling* was a chance for vendors to be forward thinking and proactive, this book serves more to put vendors on notice that buyers are starting to dictate how they want to buy and what they expect from salespeople. Their new way of buying compromises, or in some cases completely neuters, a seller's ability to influence requirements and renders traditional sales approaches blatantly in conflict with how buyers want to be treated.

It is clear why buyers have gone in this direction, but in a way it is unfortunate for both parties. For offerings of any complexity, buyers do need the help and expertise of qualified salespeople and vendors to fully understand their requirements and what it will take to implement them.

Realities of Today's Selling Environment

While we believe it is more relevant than ever, the topic of integrating sales and marketing doesn't generate much interest today. It has been discussed for more than 20 years, with minimal progress to show. Over time, people will refuse to allocate memory slots to issues that they feel cannot be addressed, especially if past efforts have proved futile. Still, the issue of integrating sales and marketing has resurfaced under another name that does generate interest: customer experience management (CEM).

The problem is that traditional approaches can't and won't address the issues of managing CEM over an entire B2B sales staff. A new approach is necessary because CEM is impossible without a defined sales process. Product marketing, marketing, and sales require rules if progress is to be made. Organizations that are successful in creating such rules will reap huge rewards through making the buying experience a competitive advantage.

There are a number of realities that present challenges to beginning to develop CEM, but vendors that want to prosper will have to acknowledge that these challenges exist and attempt to address them in tactical ways.

Senior Executive Support

We hope that you've concluded by this time that the disconnect between buyers and sellers is widening because of the way the Internet facilitates researching offerings and vendors in self-service mode. CEOs, senior executives, and boards can no longer treat sales as the elephant in the room that nobody wants to discuss. Abdication of responsibility to a VP of sales won't change the way organizations sell. Just as buyers stereotype salespeople, employees and executives of vendors do so as well. Salespeople are viewed as mercenaries, gunslingers, glad-handers, and so on. Sales has long been treated as an art rather than a science. There will always remain some art to selling, but institutionalizing a sales approach is a prerequisite for meaningful change.

Paying lip service won't create the changes that are necessary to align with buyers and begin to allow CEM. There must be a top-down commitment to implementing a process that empowers buyers, fueled by active senior executive–level involvement.

We've seen some B2B organizations create new titles and fill them with people charged with owning the customer experience. These are often staff functions that somehow have dotted-line touches with sales and marketing. To us, this is an example of recognizing a problem and applying a Band-Aid when a tourniquet is required. CEM is a noble goal to strive for, but when numbers have to be achieved, shortcuts or traditional selling approaches will be used.

Rather than create a title, we'd prefer to add responsibility for CEM to the only person who should and can own it: the CEO. While having the formal title of chief executive officer, she can also assume the responsibility of being the customer experience officer.

Building Blocks of CEM

The prerequisites for implementing a sales process are the same ones required to affect the customer buying experience. We'd like to offer some tactical approaches on how to structure them.

Sales Ready Messaging

Marketing and sales should agree upon a Targeted Conversation List of the titles that sellers must call on to sell, fund, and implement an offering that contains a menu of business goals for each title.

Questioning templates for each conversation (vertical market, title, and goal combination) that position offerings and therefore define the outcomes of a sales call are developed. The right side of the prompter includes only those parts of your offering that can help buyers achieve the goal to be discussed. Corresponding diagnostic questions for each capability are listed on the left side of the prompter. This enables consistent product positioning, realistic buyer expectations, and a more predictable buying experience.

A Common Skill Set

All sellers must have the ability to execute Sales Ready Messaging. An examination of the prompters shows that with the exception of the header information (offering, vertical market, title, and goal), this approach to developing a buyer's needs is entirely question-based. This means that

- The buyer steers the direction that the call takes based upon how he answers the questions.

- The seller offers only those capabilities that are indicated by the way the buyer answers the diagnostic questions.

- The buyer's solution must be some subset of the capabilities on the right side of the prompter.

- During the call, there is no convincing or persuading; instead, the approach is to empower buyers to achieve their goals.

Standard Debriefing Questions

Through the use of a Solution Development Prompter, the seller should be able to answer the following debriefing questions:

- The buyer's goal(s)

- The reasons that the buyer cannot achieve a goal, which are the issues on the left side of the prompter that the buyer agrees to

- The capabilities needed, which are the items on the right side of the prompter that the buyer has agreed that she wants

- The potential value to the buyer of achieving the goal that was discussed

These answers can be documented in an e-mail or letter to the buyer that includes one additional element: a request for access to other key players who are likely to be involved in making the buying decision.

All of these elements are included in a champion letter. If the buyer agrees to the content and to provide access to other key players, the sales manager can audit the letter and grade the opportunity as being at a Champion level. The opportunity remains a C while all key players are being interviewed, either in person or on the phone. All calls on each buyer should be documented, and there should be agreement that the content reflects the conversation that the seller had with him.

After all key players have been qualified, there is an attempt to qualify the opportunity. This is done by attempting to gain consensus that the committee wants to continue with its evaluation and to negotiate a sequence of events (SOE) that reflects how the buyer wants to buy.

Defined Milestones

Salespeople require a road map to navigate buyers through a buying cycle. The milestones that are defined should reflect how buyers buy, and many organizations need different sets of milestones for different types of sales. As you'll see later, a key to managing a pipeline is to have milestones that are auditable by the managers by allowing them to review correspondence with buyers.

Our recommendations for milestones are as follows:

- *Inactive* means that an account fits a company's target market and is assigned to a salesperson, but there is no current activity. A salesperson's business development efforts should focus on getting a buying cycle started by getting a targeted key player within the account to share a goal, which would advance it to the next milestone.

- *Active* indicates that contact (proactive or reactive) has been made and the customer or prospect has expressed some interest.

- *Goal shared* is the initiation of a sales cycle in CustomerCentric Selling; it indicates that a targeted key player has shared a desire to achieve at least one goal that is on the menu of business issues that the seller can help her address. This is the last milestone that sellers are allowed to grade.

- *Champion* status can be granted only by the sales manager. It is reached only after all the qualification elements have been achieved: the letter, fax, or e-mail has been sent; the buyer has agreed to the content; and the buyer is willing to provide access to key players. The sales manager must have reviewed the customer document and graded it as a C, often after a brief discussion with the salesperson.

- *Evaluating* status is also determined by the sales manager, but only after the salesperson has gained consensus from key players that further investigation of the salesperson's offering is called for, and a sequence of events has been accepted by the buying committee.

At the end of that month, the salesperson provides a copy of the cover letter and the sequence of events, and the sales manager can change the status to E if it is deemed a qualified opportunity.

Once the seller has asked for the business, the opportunity goes into one of four grades:

- *W (Win).* The seller has an order with signed documents.

- *L (Loss).* The seller is informed that the buyer will not be moving forward with him. This loss should be attributed to either "no decision" or a named competitor.

- *V (Verbal).* The buyer has committed verbally, pending finalization of the documents needed.

- *P (Proposal).* A proposal has been issued and a decision is pending.

First Touches

Going forward, an ever-increasing percentage of buying experiences will begin electronically. Until a vendor establishes credibility and a level of trust with Web site visitors, overt attempts to qualify will scare people away. Potential buyers prefer (want or demand) that early interactions be anonymous.

To align with these buyers, can your Web site

- Make people who are curious, but who are not ready to start a buying cycle, comfortable by not trying to qualify them too soon?

- Provide general information that will be helpful to a visitor, yet be relatively vendor-agnostic?

- Determine when and how to respond differently to curious buyers as they begin to get serious about evaluating offerings?

- Determine at what level (business or technical) visitors are and provide the appropriate content and Web site experiences?

- Over time, provide some help in shaping buyers' requirements based upon the objectives that they want to accomplish?

- Provide a sticky enough relationship that when they are ready to evaluate, buyers will contact your company?

- Highlight business issues that would be consistent with a Targeted Conversation List to align with marketing and sales efforts?

- Grade and track interest so that a pipeline of curious buyers can be evaluated to estimate the number of leads that will ideally flow into the opportunity funnel?

Product and Sales Training

The silos of product and sales training give individual salespeople far too much latitude in positioning offerings. Standard product training prepares B players to sound like wind-up toys as they "pitch" product to buyers. Integration of these silos lies at the foundation of CEM.

We much prefer a focus on the use of offerings to achieve high-level business objectives. When you step back, Sales Ready Messaging is a way to integrate product and sales training. Standard product training is necessary and helpful for dealing with users and lower-level people within organizations, who are much more offering-focused than those at higher levels.

At a fundamental level, senior executives have no need for a vendor's offerings. Their needs are based on the potential improvement in business results that can be gained through the use of a vendor's offering. Quite often, those executives are not users of whatever offerings are bought, which at least in part explains why 30,000-foot-elevation discussions of offerings align with what they expect from a salesperson in a 30- to 45-minute call.

For salespeople, the only thing worse than not getting access to the decision-maker level is to have an audience and not relate to that person. Leaving the content of that 30- to 45-minute call up to salespeople who have standard product training is an accident waiting to happen.

Social Networking Is Part of the Buying Process

Vendors have no way to control or "spin" the opinions provided by buyers, regardless of whether they visit your Web site, talk with a salesperson, or buy your offerings. Vendor or seller claims about quality, reliability, service, and support must be delivered if buyers are to give the vendor high marks for their buying experience and satisfaction after the sale.

Toward that end, the CEO must foster a culture that empowers people that have contact with customers to do what it takes to resolve any issues that may arise to the buyer's satisfaction. At a recent conference we attended, the discussion turned to customer service, and within a group of 25 people, two stories were shared:

- One person was having trouble with a cell phone dropping calls. While looking at it, the sales clerk realized that the screen wouldn't flip from vertical to horizontal display when it was rotated. The phone was out of warranty, and when asked, the buyer answered honestly that he didn't know if it had ever worked the way it was supposed to. Without hesitation, the sales clerk gave him a brand new phone at no charge.

- Another attendee left his cell phone in a rental car and realized that he had done so after boarding his flight home. He called the rental car company and explained the situation. The next day, the cell phone was delivered to his office via an overnight carrier.

The companies mentioned got a huge boost from these two people who shared examples of vendors going above and beyond what was expected with regard to customer care and service. This is the upside of empowering people at all levels that interface with customers to be responsive. Without having to go into detail, as you can imagine, at the break, this also elicited some horror stories of poor service. Multiply the number of people involved by thousands and you see the power of social networking.

While it is a major advantage to have customers that are delighted to do business with you, taking it to the next level requires having them be able to quantify the results that they have achieved. One way to do this is to agree prior to implementation on some baseline metrics that are likely to improve and then track them with the customer on a quarterly basis.

This approach offers many benefits beyond the ultimate goal of quantifying results:

- It ensures contact with customers every 90 days.

- If there are any issues, it means that a problem is never more than 90 days old.

- If your offering is meeting or exceeding customers' expectations, it presents an ideal opportunity to try to generate interest in other offerings.

- Quantified results can be helpful when prospects are doing a cost versus benefit analysis and are trying to estimate what improvements they can realize. .

Near the end of the buying cycle, knowing that a vendor will be there after the sale to monitor results may also help buyers mitigate their concerns about risk and finalize their buying decisions.

CRM Is Here to Stay

While they were never able to deliver on the vendors' hype, CRM systems and their successors have become necessary for most companies. Many of the unrealized benefits can be attained by implementing a repeatable sales process. Technology works best with high-quality input. We hope you appreciate that at the beginning of a pipeline, an audit of deliverables by the first-level sales manager is far more reliable than blindly accepting the opinions of sellers, who are under pressure to show a large number of accounts and high levels of activity and progress.

Another way to improve the customer buying experience is to have another look at the milestones within your CRM system.

- They will usually reflect the way you've decided you want to sell to buyers, and therefore they may be in conflict with how your buyers want to buy. Take a fresh look and see if there are modifications you can make to better align with your clients' buying processes.

- Usage and acceptance of a CRM system by salespeople is critical if it is to provide benefit to them and therefore to the executive management team. A surefire way to drain enthusiasm from salespeople is to take a "one size fits all" approach to milestones and required deliverables.

- Revisit your sales environment and consider defining separate milestones based on the size and complexity of your offerings. As a fundamental example, consider that the steps needed for a $50,000 sale will vary significantly if it represents an add-on for an exiting client or if the seller is working with a potential new account.

Salespeople will grab hold of any excuse for avoiding things that they don't want to do. Having milestones that are out of alignment with the types of opportunities they are working on makes their jobs more difficult and wastes time. In such cases, they may be right to circumvent the system.

Customer Feedback

Customer-centric vendors survey their clients on a regular basis, focusing on their offerings, support, and service. In realizing the potential value of positive buying experiences, surveying people involved in the buying committee could yield valuable information about how to better align with your buyers and could also allow further capturing of best practices as you see differences from region to region or among different salespeople.

Summary

The buying environment has changed more in the last 5 years than it did in the previous 50. This is a trend that is likely to accelerate going forward. We are at the fledgling stage of a buyer revolution fueled by years of resentment, during which vendors and salespeople have been perceived as taking advantage of buyers. As younger people advance in their careers and become responsible for making B2B buying decisions, the approaches outlined in this book will become the norm. Beyond that, we can only imagine what capabilities, new offerings, and technologies will further empower buyers.

For the first time ever, buyers are dictating the terms of their relationship with a salesperson or vendor. They are providing an outline for how they want to be treated. Vendors with the "best" product and price will lose more than their share to vendors that have a competitive price and product, but also enjoy the ability to provide superior buying experiences.

Relying on individual salespeople isn't a viable strategy. Today, superior salespeople (13 percent or less) have reacted intuitively to the changes we've described, but even they don't fully realize how the rules are changing. Quota salespeople spend far more time looking through the windshield rather than looking in their rearview mirrors and analyzing what has happened. The challenge is to institutionalize how you want the buying experience to be, from first awareness through implementation, to maximize the probability of having satisfied buyers, not only from an offering and results standpoint, but also in how they were treated during the buying cycle.

The challenge is great and is exceeded only by the potential rewards for organizations that align with buyers. Our suggestion is that you embrace the revolution and create a sales culture that facilitates buying.

It's time for you to rethink the sales cycle.

INDEX

About.com, 119
Active needs, 51-56
Active status, 223
Activity management, 182-184
Aligning with buyers, 61-64, 186-190
Amazon, 200, 205-206
Answers.com, 119
Apple Computer, 204-208
The Art of War (Tzu), 7
Awareness and urgency (stage 1):
    aligning with buyers, 61-64
    creating awareness, 57-61
    curious buyers, 56-57
    marketing versus sales, 47-51
    memory capacity, 47-51
    understanding buyer
        decision-making
        process, 51-56

Belonging-love needs, 5-6
Bezos, Jeff, 200
Bill of Rights for B2B Customers, 212-214
The Black Hole (Schmonsees), 151
Blogs:
    emergence of, 32-33
    reassurance through, 113
    research in, 80-81
    (*See also* Internet)
Bosworth, Mike, 12-13
B2B (business-to-business):
    versus B2C, 209-210
    customer's Bill of Rights, 212-214
    (*See also specific topics*)
B2C (business-to-consumer), 209-210
Business buyer influences, 83
Business-to-business (B2B):
    versus B2C, 209-210

customer's Bill of Rights, 212-214
    (*See also specific topics*)
Business-to-consumer (B2C), 209-210
Buyer behavior:
    aligning selling approaches
        with, 82-85
    changes with risk, 127-132
    defined, xiii, 83
    human, 12-13, 132-134
Buyers:
    aligning selling approaches
        with behavior of, 82-85
    aligning with, 61-64, 186-190
    categories of, 51
    concerns/objections of, 151
    curious, 56-57
    customer service and support, 118
    early market, 162-163
    feedback, 228
    how they buy, 13-23
    people buying from people, 91-94
    power of:
        buyer's revenge, 27-42
        odd couple, 3-26
        understanding decision-
            making process, xi-xiii
    quest for control by, 8-12
    responding to cold calls, 37-38
    revenge:
        buying phases, 38-40
        current buying trends, 36-37
        Internet blogs, 32-33
        Internet development, 28-30
        Internet search engines, 30-31
        response to cold calls, 37-38

Buyers' revenge *(Cont'd.)*
  social networking, 33-36
  understanding decision-making
      process, xi-xiii, 51-56
  unhappy, 206-207
  view of seller by, 6-8
"Buying curves," 13
Buying cycle/process:
  current trends in, 36-37
  forming preferences, 92-94
  influences on decisions, 84-85
  managing sales to facilitate, 177-
      197
  phases of, 13-23
  versus sales cycle, 151
  social networking, 226-227
  stage 1: awareness and urgency,
      45-66
    aligning with buyers, 61-64
    creating awareness, 57-61
    curious buyers, 56-57
    marketing versus sales, 48-51
    memory capacity, 47-51
    understanding buyer
        decision-making process,
        51-56
  stage 2: research, 67-88
    aligning selling approaches
        with buyer behavior, 82-85
    Internet, 75-82
    pre-Internet, 69-75
    sales plan, 85-88
  stage 3: preferences, 89-104
    determining, 98-100
    forming, 92-94
    live sales contact, 94-95
    people buying from people,
        91-94
    sales plan, 102-103
    salespeople ruining
        opportunities, 101
    salespeople status, 96-98
  stage 4: reassurance, 105-122
    driving influences for, 113-115
    funding, 115-119
    researching, 111-113

  sales plan, 119-121
  timing versus urgency, 108-110
  stage 5: risk and buying
      decision, 123-138
    B2B, 125-127
    changes with risk, 127-132
    doomed proposals, 134-137
    human buying behavior, 132-
        134
    traditional selling conflicts with,
        141-153
Buying decision and risk (stage 5),
    123-138
  B2B, 125-127
  changes with risk, 127-132
  doomed proposals, 134-137
  human buying behavior, 132-
      134

Champion level, 191-193, 222-223
Closing techniques, 144-146
Cold calls, 37-38
Commitment phase, 15-23
Common skill set, 221-222
Competitive advantages:
  achieving with sales process,
      215-229
  as fleeting, ix-x
Consumer behavior (*See* Buyer
    behavior)
Control, quest for, 8-12
Coordination, lack of, 148-150
Creating awareness, 57-61
Customer experience management
    (CEM):
  building blocks of, 221-227
  common skill set, 221-222
  in current selling environment,
      219-220
  first touches, 224-225
  milestones, 223-224
  overview, 167-168
  product/sales training, 225
  sales ready messaging, 221
  standard debriefing questions,
      222

Customer relationship management
    (CRM), 227-228
Customer service and support, 118
Customer solution marketing
    (CSM), 156-157
CustomerCentric Messaging Matrix,
    63-64
CustomerCentric Selling, 209-210,
    218-219
Customers (See Buyers)

Deal versus transaction, 151
Debriefing questions, 190-192, 222
Decision to buy and risk (stage 5),
    123-138
    B2B, 125-127
    changes with risk, 127-132
    doomed proposals, 134-137
    human buying behavior, 132-
        134
Dell, ix
Determining buyer preferences, 98-
    100
Developing:
    MAGIC moments, 210-212
    offerings, 157-159
    products, 149-150
Disney, x
Disruptive offerings, 161-163
Driving influences for reassurance,
    113-115

Early market buyers, 162-163
Einstein, Albert, 144
Employees, unhappy, 206-207
End user influences, 83
Evaluating status, 223
Evaluation phase, 13-23

Fedex, 206
Feedback from customers, 228
Formal sales process, 181-182
Formalizing sales organization,
    163-167
Forrester Group, 111-112
Funding, 115-116

"Global Faces and Networked
    Places" (Nielsen
    BuzzMetric), 113
Goal shared status, 223
Google, 178-179, 206

Hard Facts, Dangerous Half-Truths
    and Total Nonsense
    (Sutton & Pfeffer), 107
Hardware as a service (HaaS), 207-
    208
Hierarchy of Needs (Maslow), 5-6

IBM, 178
Inactive status, 223
Infrastructure staff member
    influences, 83
Interest qualification (IQ), 187
Internet:
    blogs, 32-33, 80-81, 113
    development of, 28-30
    pre-Internet research, 69-75
    research, 75-82
    search engines, 30-31
    social networking, 33-36, 79-81,
        113, 226-227

Jobs, Steve, 207

Kenmore Pro, 201-204

L (Loss) grade, 224
Latent needs, 51-56
Law of Buyer's Assurance, 110
Leveraging technology, 150
Levitt, Theodore, 53
LinkedIn, 119
Live sales contact, 94-95
Losses to NDI (No Decision, Inc.),
    132
Lovaglia, Michael (professor), 106-
    108

MAGIC moments in customer
    experience:
    Apple Computer, 204-208

B2B customer's Bill of Rights, 212-214
B2B versus B2C, 209-210
Sears, 201-204
steps to developing, 210-212
unhappy employees and unhappy customers, 206-207
what makes, 205-206
Managing:
activity, 182-184
components, 180-181
sales pipeline process, 190-197
sales to facilitate buying process, 177-197
Marketing:
adopting culture of, 120
versus sales, 48-51
tactical, 174
(*See also* Product marketing; Sales; Salespeople)
Maslow, Abraham, Hierarchy of Needs, 5-6
Memory capacity, 47-51
Messaging, as a foundation, 184-185
Midlevel manager influences, 83
Milestones, 223-224
Moore, Geoffrey, 162-163

Needs:
buyer perception of, 51-56
development phase, 13-23
New York Times, 200
Nielsen BuzzMetric, 113

Offerings:
developing, 157-159
disruptive, 161-163

P (Proposal) grade, 224
Pfeffer, Jeffrey, 107
Physiological needs, 5-6
Preferences (stage 3):
defined, 90
determining, 98-100

forming, 92-94
live sales contact, 94-95
people buying from people, 91-94
sales plan, 102-103
salespeople ruining opportunities, 101
salespeople status, 96-98
Pre-Internet research, 69-75
Product development, 149-150
Product marketing:
customer experience management (CEM), 167-168
developing, 157-159
disruptive offerings, 161-163
formalizing sales organization, 163-167
overview, 156-157
process foundation, 168-175
variations in, 159-161
Product training, 147-148, 225
Professional services, importance of, 118
Proof phase, 13-23
Proposals, doomed, 134-137
"Put Buyers First? What a Concept" *(New York Times),* 200

Questions, debriefing, 190-192, 222

Reassurance (stage 4):
driving influences for, 113-115
funding, 115-119
researching, 111-113
sales plan, 119-121
timing versus urgency, 108-110
Research (stage 2):
aligning selling approaches with buyer behavior, 82-85
with blogs, 80-81
Internet, 75-82
pre-Internet, 69-75
reassurance, 111-113
sales plan, 85-88
Risk and buying decision (stage 5):
B2B, 125-127

changes with risk, 127-132
doomed proposals, 134-137
human buying behavior, 132-134

Safety needs, 5-6
Sales:
adopting culture of, 120
managing pipeline process, 190-197
managing to facilitate buying process, 177-197
versus marketing, 48-51
profession, 146-147
training in, 225
(*See also* Marketing; Salespeople)
Sales culture, facilitating buying behavior through:
MAGIC moments in customer experience, xi, 199-214
product marketing, 155-176
sales management and buying process, 177-198
sales process for competitive advantage, x-xi, 215-230
traditional selling vs. new buying, 141-154
Sales cycle/process:
achieving sustainable competitive advantages with, 215-229
versus buying cycle, 151
grades of, 224
importance of formal, 181-182
managing pipeline, 190-197
understanding decision-making process, xiv
Sales management:
aligning with expert buyers, 186-190
components of, 180-181
formal sales process, 181-182
managing activity, 182-184
managing sales pipeline process, 190-197

messaging, 184-185
Sales organization, 163-167
Sales plan:
preference phase, 102-103
reassurance, 119-120
research phase, 85-88
Sales ready messaging:
creation of, 174-175
overview, 184-185, 209-210
product/sales training, 225
as a skill, 221-222
Salesforce.com (SFDC), 159-161
Salespeople:
debriefing questions for, 190-192
defined, 174
professional status of, 96-98
ruining opportunities, 101
(*See also* Marketing; Sales)
Schmonsees, Bob, 151
Search engines, 30-31
Sears, 201-204
Self-actualization needs, 5-6
Self-esteem needs, 5-6
Seller:
buyer's view of, 6-8
quest for control by, 8-12
(*See also* Vendor)
Selling:
closing techniques, 144-146
conflicts between traditional and new buying process, 141-153
realities of today's environment, 219-220
Senior executive support, 220-221
Sequence of events (SOE), 193-197, 222
Skill set, common, 221-222
Social networking:
overview, 33-36
as part of buying process, 226-227
reassurance through, 113
research in, 79-81
"Social Technographics® of Business Buyers, The" (Forrester Group), 111-112

Software as a service (SaaS):
    benefits of, 115-116
    prevalence of, 159-161
Solution development phase, 13-23
Solution Development Prompter,
    188-190, 222
*Solution Selling: Creative Buyers in
    Difficult Selling Markets*
    (Bosworth), 12-13
Standard debriefing questions, 222
Supply chain competency, xi
Sutton, Robert, 107

Tactical marketing, 174
TCL (targeted conversation list),
    168-175, 221
Technology, leveraging, 150
3M, 206
Timing versus urgency, 108-110
Toyota, 206
Traditional selling:
    closing techniques, 144-146
    conflicts with new buying
        process, 141-153
    lack of coordination, 148-150
    product training, 147-148
    sales profession, 146-147
    vocabulary changes, 151-152
Training:
    product, 147-148, 225
    sales, 225
Transaction versus deal, 151
Tzu, Sun, 7

Unhappy employees/customers,
    206-207

Urgency:
    and awareness (stage 1), 45-66
        aligning with buyers, 61-64
        creating awareness, 57-61
        curious buyers, 56-57
        marketing versus sales, 48-51
        memory capacity, 47-51
        understanding buyer
            decision-making process,
            51-56
    sense of, 108-110
Usage scenario, 170

V (Verbal) grade, 224
"Value propositions," 133
Vendor:
    importance of stability of, 118
    vocabulary changes for
        organizations, 151-152
    (*See also* Seller)
Vocabulary, changes in, 151-152

W (Win) grade, 224
WalMart, xi
WCSOs (world-class
        organizations), 50-51, 99-
        100
Web sites, 224-225

XCS (Xerox Computer Services),
    12-13

Yahoo! Answers, 119
Young, Tim, 201-204
Y2K, 108

ABOUT THE AUTHORS

John Holland

Leveraging over 20 years' experience in sales, sales management, and consulting, John Holland coauthored and cofounded CustomerCentric Selling® (CCS) in 2002. His primary responsibility is continuing to evolve CCS intellectual property to reflect ongoing changes in the buying habits of people and organizations.

Prior to launching CCS, as a sales consultant Holland helped organizations design and implement standardized sales processes in such diverse sectors as professional services, technology, leasing, overnight delivery, logistics, language localization, office equipment, temporary housing, and financial services.

In 2003, Holland teamed with Mike Bosworth, who originally authored *Solution Selling*, to coauthor *CustomerCentric Selling*. In 2007, Holland coauthored *Relational Capital* with Ed Wallace.

John has had articles published in *Sales and Marketing Executive Report*, *Selling Power* magazine and the *American Marketing Association* (AMA). He has spoken on various topics for organizations such as SMEI, IIDMA, AMA, and Software Success. John serves as a participant in CustomerThink's panel of experts and Cognizant's Customer Advisory Board.

Holland earned a degree in mechanical engineering from Northeastern University before starting his career with IBM's General Systems division. John delivers keynote speeches and serves on the advisory boards of a limited number of companies, providing guidance on product direction, service offerings, and overall sales and tactical marketing strategies.

Tim Young

Tim joined CustomerCentric Selling® in 2007 as CEO. Bringing his vast business experience to the global sales process improvement firm,

Tim's primary focus is on building the CustomerCentric Selling® brand and its global network of business partners.

Tim began his business career with Advo Systems in 1979 before joining Harte-Hanks Communications in 1982. During a 13-year career, Tim rose to the rank of president of Harte-Hanks Marketing Services, a position he held for eight years, where he spearheaded the launch and rapid growth of the firm's highly profitable global Customer Relationship Management business.

In 1995, Tim founded TECHMAR Communications as a provider of sales and marketing support services. Within five years, the company grew from a one-person start-up to over 450 employees with facilities in six countries. *Inc.* magazine recognized TECHMAR in 2001 as the one-hundred-thirtieth fastest growing privately held business in the United States.

In his personal life, Tim serves as a founding member of the board of advisors of the National Kidney Registry and has a passion for sustainable farming, where he and his wife, Liz, operate Nature's Harmony Farm in Georgia.

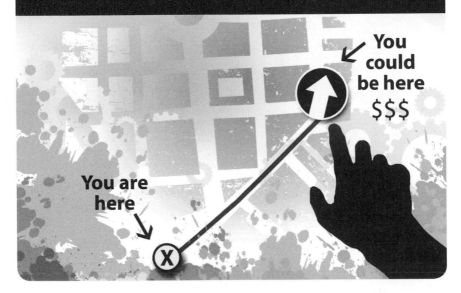